Corporate Environmental Management 3

Towards Sustainable Development

Richard Welford

Earthscan Publications Ltd, London

For Philip Yong

No Self, No Other

Only Karma

First published in the UK in 2000 by
Earthscan Publications Ltd

Copyright © Richard Welford, 2000

A catalogue record for this book is available from the British Library

ISBN: 1 85383 641 9 paperback
        1 85383 660 5 hardback

Typsetting by PCS Mapping & DTP
Printed and bound in Great Britain by Biddles Ltd
www.biddles.co.uk
Cover design by Andrew Corbett

For a full list of publications please contact:

Earthscan Publications Ltd
120 Pentonville Road
London, N1 9JN, UK
Tel: +44 (0)20 7278 0433
Fax: +44 (0)20 7278 1142
Email: earthinfo@earthscan.co.uk
http://www.earthscan.co.uk

Earthscan is an editorially independent subsidiary of Kogan Page Ltd and
publishes in association with WWF-UK and the International Institute for
Environment and Development

This book is printed on elemental chlorine-free paper

Contents

List of Figures and Tables

FIGURES

TABLES

Acronyms and Abbreviations

CIA	Chemical Industries Association
EIA	environmental impact assessment
EPE	environmental performance evaluation
GATT	General Agreement on Tariffs and Trade
GNP	gross national product
IMF	International Monetary Fund
ISO	International Organization for Standardization
LCA	life-cycle assessment
LCC	life-cycle cost
NGO	non-governmental organization
OECD	Organisation for Economic Co-operation and Development
QFD	quality function deployment
TNCs	transnational corporations
WTO	World Trade Organization

Preface

This is the third and final book in a trilogy on corporate environmental management. The first book, *Corporate Environmental Management 1: Systems and Strategies*, examined management tools and techniques which could be implemented by business in order to improve its environmental performance. The second book, *Corporate Environmental Management 2: Culture and Organisations*, argued that no technique or technology can be entirely successful without considering the human element.

This final book takes as its theme: 'Towards Sustainable Development'. It is much more tentative than the previous two books, and begins to explore certain issues rather than put forward definitive answers – such is the nature of sustainable development, of course. Although this book does have a structure, it is not rigid and in many ways the chapters are better read as stand-alone papers. To the extent to which there is an order in the chapters, however, I begin by looking at business and society (Chapter 1), progress to business and ethics (Chapter 2) before considering the huge conflicts and contradictions facing us when we examine business in the context of the international economic order and globalization (Chapter 3).

Over the years, however, I have come to believe that the primary problem facing the world is not excessive production but excessive consumption. Businesses somewhere in the world are always going to produce the goods that are demanded by people, if they can do so at a profit. Thus a theme running through the remaining four chapters is that we really have to deal with consumption that is often addictive and psychotic rather than utility maximizing. Chapter 4 examines how we might expect businesses to get involved in managing both production and consumption. Chapter 5 looks at the issues of marketing and communications and sees a significant role for business in the areas of education and campaigning.

The final two chapters are much more personal than any of the other materials presented in these three books. They take a more spiritual approach to dealing with issues of environmental damage and sustainable development. Somewhat surprisingly to me, a number of business people who saw drafts of this material were enthusiastic about it and in at least one case it triggered some very deep and heart-felt emotions. In Chapter 6, I map out one possible path to the achievement of some sort of sustainable development, using some basic ideas from Buddhist thought. In my view, despite what I have written before, such an approach increasingly seems to me to be the only way forward if we are to create a sustainable, just and civilized planet on which to live.

In Chapter 7 I go further in suggesting that business has to go through some fundamental change if it is to survive, but that that change has to be personal, involving the managers who guide our businesses. I do however see some signs of willingness on the part of individuals to do this. More and more of my friends are re-evaluating how they live and work, and I too am now stepping out of the competitive rat race.

I hope that my contributions in the field of corporate environmental management have had, and continue to have, an influence on the thinking of both business managers and researchers working in this field. I have to fight my humility and let my ego take over for a while when I say that I think they have. I hope you agree. Please forgive this book if it seems raw at times, but we must now move forward, and here I try to open up the eyes of readers to the next revolution: the rediscovery of spirituality.

Richard Welford
March 2000

Chapter 1

Towards Sustainable Development in a Postmodern Society

INTRODUCTION

Tackling sustainable development from the perspective of the firm is not an easy task. To talk of a sustainable company is perhaps meaningless, because however big or small the organization, it cannot be seen in isolation from the society in which it operates. However, it may be possible to talk of a business acting in a way which is consistent with sustainable development. Indeed this is what this book seeks to demonstrate, along with some of the tools and policies which can help to achieve a more sustainable business. As a starting point, therefore, it is important to consider the concept of sustainable development in the context of broader societal dimensions. But we need also to examine a range of issues (many of which are contradictory) that are inherent in sustainable development. These include issues of ethics, debates around globalization and free trade, the thorny issue of consumption and marketing, as well as the more spiritual dimensions of environmentalism.

There can be little doubt that the waves of social and environmental concern which we have seen over the last 30 years have revolved around an upward trend. In the 1990s those real concerns became so great that legislators, regulators, policy-makers and some intergovernmental organizations have given environmental considerations their proper place among all the other competing objectives of a modern pluralist society. Different stakeholders and non-governmental organizations (NGOs) have championed various objectives which they see as necessary parts of sustainable development.

Businesses have responded in many different ways. Many have been resistant to change, others have been accommodating and some have been increasingly proactive. A small minority have even become champions themselves, showing what can be achieved by searching for social and environmental excellence.

Like the two previous titles in this series, this book is unashamedly about reform, but it is argued throughout that that reform must be more radical than the piecemeal approaches that we have seen to date. Indeed the concept of sustainable development is a radical concept, requiring as it does every organization and every person to think in time dimensions longer than a generation and placing an emphasis on both rights and responsibilities. Some may still argue that reformist efforts merely forestall the impending collapse of the industrial economies, a collapse which may need to occur before the real work of reconstruction can begin (Tokars, 1987). That may indeed be the case, but this book argues that there are significant reforms which businesses can and should adopt that may avoid this impending doom. Ostensibly that reform has to revolve around the fundamental ways in which we do business, in which the capitalist system forces businesses to operate, and in the organization of enterprises which are responsible for so much damage to date.

As a starting point we need to recognize that the issues surrounding human life and economic activity are an interdependent part of wider social and ecological processes that sustain life on earth. We must interact with these processes in a sustainable way or they will bring about, in turn, the demise of present societies. That requires fundamental reforms of the structures and processes which have caused the problem in the first place. That means finding new ways of doing business, of including workers in change processes, of organizing trade so as to protect the developing world and indigenous populations, and of sustaining all other life forms on the planet.

What is being advocated in the chapters that follow, therefore, may seem controversial to some, but there is a fundamental need to examine and redefine some of the sacred tenets of traditional economic thought. We cannot rely on established structures, technology and science to bring about real change. They have not done so to date. There is a need for a more radical rethink of many of the issues which face society and, as part of that, we need to think carefully about enterprise culture. What nobody can provide, however, is a formula for the way in which societies must operate into the future. When Karl Marx was once asked to describe what a communist society would look like, he replied that he could not write recipes for the cookshops of the future. We can point, however, to the inadequacies of current environmental strategies and to the directions along which organizations must tread. We can provide a series of suggestions and demands for business and hope sincerely that there will be sufficient societal pressure to further encourage the business community to take more steps forward.

One thing is sure, however, and that is that we can no longer rely on science and technology to dig us out of the holes which we have created. When in 1798 Thomas Malthus warned that the population was growing so fast that it would eventually outstrip food supply, technology rescued us in the form of fertilizers and refrigeration. Now as the world population rises to six billion and beyond, Malthusian voices are raised again but their faith in the technological fix has deserted them. Moreover, the science and technology which initially provided deliverance now leads to sick plants with inadequate resistance to pests, to water contaminated by the pesticides which were supposed to put that problem right, to genetic modification with unknown consequences and to desertification and erosion. This book does not represent a doctrine of despair. It does, however, encourage the reader to think more widely about the environmental strategies which we need to pursue in order to bring about an end to the mounting degradation of the planet.

THE CHALLENGE OF SUSTAINABLE DEVELOPMENT AND CONSEQUENCES FOR BUSINESS STRATEGY

Social and environmental concerns are not particularly new – they have been a matter of public concern for over a quarter of a century. As scientific and technical knowledge relating to the causes and effects of environmental damage has become more complete, the pressure to change the ways in which industry behaves has increased. Individuals are also changing their patterns of behaviour and industry is having to respond to the seemingly endless demands of the new, environmentally aware consumer. Indeed, such are the wide-ranging pressures being put on business from a range of diverse stakeholders that increasingly business will have to account for its actions if it is going to survive in the marketplace. With increased information availability, more sophisticated targeting of companies by pressure groups and a greater wish to see companies as good corporate citizens, the very strategy of a business has to be sensitive to increasing social and environmental demands.

In its early stages the environmental debate in industry was largely one of rhetoric rather than action. More recently, businesses have recognized the need to improve their environmental performance, but we have still not seen any radical shift in business practices as a whole that are capable of bringing about a lasting reversal of trends towards environmental destruction. This is compounded by the process of globalization which blurs the frontiers of a single business' activities. While it is difficult for industry to refute the general need for environmental protection, its response has too often been piecemeal, adopting bolt-on strategies aimed at fine-tuning its environmental performance within the traditional constraints imposed by a traditional capitalist society. To date there have been many publications aimed at telling businesses how they can achieve a measure of environmental improvement (and now many which talk of the need for social accountability), but there has been rather less debate about the very way in which they operate which will lead to real progress. There is a need to develop practical solutions to meet the challenge of sustainable development. However, it must be recognized that those solutions mean re-evaluating the very basis on which we do business.

Traditionally the view of the corporate world has been based on the idea that the investments and innovations of industry drive economic growth and satisfy the demands of the consumer. However, in doing so, be it because of the resources that they consume, the processes that they apply or the products that they manufacture, business activity has become a major contributor to environmental destruction (Welford and Gouldson, 1993). Many commentators have argued that we need to find new technologies and develop more efficient methods of production. But the very basis of that argument needs to be examined carefully. Growth can no longer be a sole objective which stands alone and pays no heed to its environmental consequences now and into the future. Growth is only justifiable if it is associated with development which in itself needs to concentrate more directly on equity. We know that the technological solution is insufficient in itself, and we cannot assume that science and technology will cure the wrongs of the past and provide a new growth path. There is a need for a change in attitudes toward both consumption and production. Moreover, there is a need to look closely at the ethics of business and to discover new forms of industrial organization and culture which, while they exist in a broad free-market framework with due regulation, promote development and equity into the future.

For a long time now neoclassical economists have told us that, if harnessed correctly, the market mechanism can be utilized to develop the solutions which are so vital if the environment is to be protected. But the free market to date has failed to bring about equitable distributions of income; it has failed to protect the developing world and has done little to protect the planet. Moreover, the market solution depends on cooperation between governments, which must provide fiscal incentives for environmental improvement, industry and consumers. But each of these agencies has competing objectives and, often, competing values. In particular, industry to date has been driven by profitability, and while that profitability might be seen as vital to economic growth, we should begin to demand that industry puts ethical objectives, such as environmental improvement and sustainable development, into its strategic plan. Reliance on the market mechanism alone is likely to be insufficient to bring about real improvement. That is not to suggest that it has no role, but that it needs to be supplemented by changes in corporate culture based on a commitment to see long-term environmental improvement and equitable development. These are the challenges for industry which are posed by the concept of sustainable development – a concept to which, to date, much of industry has only paid lip-service.

Business strategy therefore has to embrace the concept of sustainable development. This is going to be a difficult task, because at times that concept may not be entirely consistent with other strategies, such as growth, profit maximization and the creation shareholder value and investment. Of course, conflict will not always occur: the number of stories of companies reducing their costs through the adoption of traditional environmental management principles is now so overwhelming that one is left wondering why every company is not doing it. But where conflict does occur, businesses have choices to make. Those will be difficult choices and companies will have to think carefully about the consequences of their decisions. The bottom line, however, is that ultimately it will be the senior managers who will have to choose. There will be little which many of us can do about it. However, what we can expect is that businesses will become increasingly transparent and accountable in their strategic decision-making and will then be able to explain to stakeholders why they took one path rather than another.

Ultimately, the most we can expect of businesses is that they make their values clear. Based on an assessment of these values and a similar assessment of their actions, we as consumers and citizens can decide whether we want to do business with them. With the common usage of the Internet, information about companies is increasingly available and we have seen campaigners against organizations such as McDonalds and Shell use this medium to rather good effect. In both the so-called McLibel case and Shell's embarrassment over the sinking of the *Brent Spar* and its activities in Nigeria, the image of the company (and one can only assume its long-term profitability) were compromised. In both cases it was the arrogance of the company's business strategy that ultimately led to problems for them.

SUSTAINABLE DEVELOPMENT AND IMPLICATIONS FOR INDUSTRY

We now have a range of commentators explaining that the continuing ability of the environment to supply raw materials and assimilate waste while maintaining biodiversity and a quality of life is being increasingly undermined. If growth and development are to take on new, responsible paths we have to find a way of doing it that will not further degrade the environment in which we live and not create many of the social tensions which we now observe. In its simplest form, sustainable development is defined in the Brundtland Report as development that meets the needs of the present generation without compromising the ability of future generations to meet their own needs (World Commission on Environment and Development, 1987). Such a simple statement has profound implications. It implies that, as a minimum, all human activity must refrain from causing any degree of permanent damage through its consumption of environmental resources. But it also implies that we need to create social infrastructures which are capable of handling at least the doubling of the world's population over the next century.

As an ultimate objective, the concept of sustainability is immensely valuable. However, strategies are needed to translate conceptual theories into practical reality. This requires a more radical assessment of environmental strategy than we have seen to date. The challenge that faces the economic system is how to continue to fulfil its vital role within modern society while ensuring sustainable development. The emphasis to date has been on piecemeal moves towards sustainable development and, although this move is in the right direction, it lacks the sense of urgency and commitment which is required. There is a need to assess carefully how development can be made sustainable and this implies acceptance of the view that not all growth and development will be good. We must accept that sustainability is not something that will be achieved overnight, and that in the longer-term entire economies and individual businesses need to look towards a new type of development and growth. This in turn requires them to look at their own ethics, their objectives and their own forms of organization, corporate culture and communication.

One major obstacle which prevents sustainability from being achieved is the overall level of consumption experienced in the Western world. Consumers who are relatively wealthy seem reluctant to significantly reduce their own levels of consumption. While increasingly governments are adopting economic instruments such as taxes, subsidies and product labelling schemes to reduce and channel consumption towards more environmentally friendly alternatives, there is also a need for education among consumers. In addition, though, industry has a role to play in educating its customers and suppliers, and all businesses must be encouraged to increase further their own internal environmental efficiency by reassessing the very ways in which they do business and measuring and assessing their environmental performance.

The fact that lies behind the concept of sustainable development is that there is a trade-off between continuous economic growth and the sustainability of the environment. Over time, through greater and greater exploitation, growth causes pollution and atmospheric damage, disrupts traditional ways of living (particularly in the developing world), destroys ecosystems and feeds more and more power into oligopolistic industrial structures. The concept of sustainable development stresses the interdependence between economic growth and environmental quality, but it also goes further in demonstrating that the future is uncertain unless we can deal with the issues of equity and inequality throughout the world. It is possible to make development and environmental protection compatible and to begin to deal with the problems caused by a lack of consideration of equity issues by following sustainable strategies and by not developing the particular areas of economic activity that are most damaging to the environment and its inhabitants.

The Brundtland Report argued that economic development and environmental protection could be made compatible, but that this would require quite radical changes in economic practices throughout the world. Mass consumption is not possible indefinitely and if society today acts as if all non-renewable resources are plentiful, eventually there will be nothing left for the future. But more importantly than that, mass consumption may cause such irreparable damage that humans may not even be able to live on the planet in the future.

Not everybody accepts that the Brundtland conceptualization of sustainable development is the best one. Others, such as Daly (1996), question the emphasis on growth, pointing out that growth (a quantitative increase in output) is simply not the same as development (a qualitative improvement in people's lives). Moreover, it is argued that in many cases growth has not led to development, but rather to a significant decrease in the quality of human life. Daly argues that if sustainable development means anything, it demands that we conceive of the economy as part of the ecosystem and, as a result, give up on the ideal of economic growth. Moreover, for development to be truly sustainable it is argued that there is a need for the significant redistribution of wealth, power and economic resources from North to South.

Thus it must be stressed that there is not a single definition of sustainable development. This is not a problem if we see the concept not as something which has to be defined precisely, but as a process. There is a fruitless search for a universal definition of sustainable development; what is more important is that we begin to move towards a development path which is environmentally and socially responsible. At least in part, this means treating economics, social issues and environmental issues not as three separate and indistinguishable concepts which have to be managed, but seeing each as an important part of a larger whole. Often good business (in traditional terms) is environmentally friendly and socially responsible, but perhaps more often there are conflicts which will have to be resolved.

It seems clear, therefore, that industry must seek to provide the services demanded by consumers with the minimum social and environmental impact at all stages. This is a far-reaching challenge as it involves a reformulation not only of production processes but of the products themselves. While many consumers may be unwilling to reduce the overall levels of consumption to which they have become accustomed, they have proved willing to select the goods which produce a reduced environmental impact. Companies need to focus their environmental strategies and subsequent green marketing campaigns on supplying goods with a sustainable differential advantage. In so doing, the producer has to accept responsibility for the environmental impact of the materials and processes used at the production stage, and for the final product and its disposal. In many ways, therefore, industry has to take on a whole range of new responsibilities towards protecting the environment.

Sustainable development is not only about the direct impact on the environment, however, and a corporate strategy which deals with narrow environmental performance measures is inadequate. A key part of the concept (which is often conveniently ignored by industry) relates to equity issues. The massive inequality in wealth and standards of living which is displayed across the world makes sustainable development harder to achieve. Those living in the developing world often aspire to the standards of living of the West and we know from an environmental stance that such aspirations are presently not achievable. But what right does the West have to deny other human beings development in the same unsustainable way in which they themselves have developed? Therefore we can see that environmental improvement is inextricably linked to the wider issues of global concern which do need to be addressed. Equity has also to be tackled at the level of the firm, however. New forms of industrial organization should seek to empower workers and increase their decision-making powers, to increase democracy in the workplace and to share profits with the workforce, alongside improving environmental performance. This demands a more holistic and ethical approach to doing business which values workers as an integral and valuable part of the organization rather than a resource to be hired and fired as external market conditions change.

THE CORPORATE RESPONSE TO SUSTAINABLE DEVELOPMENT

Environmental legislation in most industrialized economies is increasingly plugging the gaps which allow environmental degradation to happen, and firms (and their directors) that attempt to hide their illegal pollution are now subject to severe penalties. Even before then, though, businesses should recognize that it is not only ethical to be environmentally friendly, but with the growth of consumer awareness in the environmental area, it will also be 'good business' in a more traditional sense. But now attention is also switching to the social concerns highlighted by the concept of sustainable development, and industry is beginning to feel pressure from a number of its stakeholders to demonstrate that it is a good corporate citizen.

Firms clearly have a role to play in the development of substitutes for non-renewable resources and innovations which reduce waste and use energy more efficiently. They also have a role in processing those materials in a way which brings about environmental improvements, and they clearly now have a role in shaping societies and in helping to produce a good social infrastructure. Many companies are politically powerful, some might say even more powerful than many of the governments around the world. Such power can be a harness for good, and sometimes it is. However, huge transnational corporations (TNCs) are often cited as creating large degrees of social unrest and conflicts in countries where they operate. This is particularly true with regard to the operations of such firms outside their Western 'homes'. Accusations of human rights abuses, corruption and cosy relationships with military dictators do not fit easily with the type of social responsibility which is demanded by the concept of sustainable development.

Within the pluralist society in which we live, a whole range of pressures are beginning to create the preconditions which are necessary to encourage businesses to respond to the environmental challenge. Industry is beginning to develop the new technologies and techniques which may help to move the global economy towards sustainability and, while accepting that the answer will not lie in technology alone, we must continue to do so. The rapid growth of public environmental awareness in recent years has also placed new pressures on industry. These pressures can take many forms as individuals collectively exercise their environmental conscience as customers, employees, investors, voters, neighbours and responsible citizens. But it is perhaps the NGO movement and its ability to expose industrial actions that is most interesting. In general, the growth of a 'civil society' means that industry may not have the power in the future which it has now. Often referred to as the 'second superpower', civil society, aided by the type of information availability which we have already discussed, has the potential to mitigate the excesses of business. This has to be seen as a good thing and businesses will have to be prepared to tackle this new force. To do so is simple: it requires companies to be more transparent, more accountable and more honest.

A strategy for responding to the demands of sustainable development must therefore begin with real commitment on the part of the whole organization. This may mean a change in corporate culture, and management has an important role to play. In leading that commitment and laying out the organization's corporate objectives with respect to social and environmental issues, management has to be the catalyst for change. Indeed it needs to rethink its whole rationale and reassess the very structures in its own organization which act as impediments to change. Moreover, change has to be on-going and management must be ever mindful of the full range of (often competing) objectives to which it is subject. Management has to find compromise between these objectives if they conflict, and design corporate strategies which are operational, consistent and achievable. Change will have to be addressed in a systematic way, dealing with the company as a whole rather than in a compartmentalized way. There is also a need to look towards the 'larger picture' rather than be driven by product-specific considerations. Moreover, corporate structures should not be seen as rigid, and the identification and development of corporate strengths should not be considered to be more important than the continuation of 'business as usual'. When it comes to the integration of social and environmental considerations, cooperative strategies need also to be considered. All too often competition has been the dominant ideology in business, but increasingly cooperative strategies between businesses and involving the public and regulatory agencies can bring about benefits. Single-minded competitive strategies run the risk of isolating businesses from new developments, expertise and public opinion, which are invaluable to the socially and environmentally aware company.

SUSTAINABLE DEVELOPMENT IN AN INTERNATIONAL CONTEXT

One of the characteristics of post-war Europe has been the growing integration associated with European economic union. But more recently, that trend has been mirrored in other parts of the world. International trade is dominated by the global triad of Europe, North America and Japan, and all countries belonging to the Organisation for Economic Co-operation and Development (OECD) have found their economies becoming more interdependent and interrelated through the growth of trade, technology transfer and global communications networks. Through the mass media it has often been models of Western consumer culture which have been relayed across the planet and into the developing world. Yet global inequality persists between the higher income and lower income countries and there are considerable differences within the lower income countries themselves.

In many ways, no country can see itself as independent. The global spread of industrial activity, along with the expansion of information systems, means that no country can insulate itself from its external economic climate. Neither can countries insulate themselves from the growing pollution and social disruption caused by industrialization and consumerism. Perhaps most intrusive, however, are the activities of TNCs which bring with them their own corporate cultures, dominate international trade and production, and are therefore to be held responsible for significant levels of transnational environmental damage. In the decade between 1980 and 1990 the Worldwatch Institute has estimated that gross world output of goods and services grew from US$4.5 trillion to US$20 trillion, and international trade grew by approximately 4 per cent per year (Brown, 1991). This sort of trend continued during the 1990s.

The rapid evolution of an international economic system has not been matched by international political integration or international laws to regulate that system. The consequence is that many TNCs are effectively allowed to operate above the law, above national boundaries, and are able to set their own international economic agenda. Moreover, by creating a situation where many developing world countries are dependent on their patronage, employment and technology, they often wield considerable political power as well. This is hardly a scenario which can be reconciled with sustainable development.

Since the 1980s we have seen an increasing move towards the liberal market version of the capitalist economy. By the beginning of the 1990s many former Communist countries were putting radical and austere policies in place to introduce a market mechanism into their economies and to privatize previously state-run companies. More recently we have seen the virtual collapse of many economies (including those of Indonesia and Russia) and this has led to tremendous human suffering and social conflict. But the governments of developing countries are still attracted towards the liberal free-market model, seeing it as the system which is able to deliver the goods and raise general levels of material prosperity. Where developing countries have been wary of adopting *laissez-faire* economic policies, they have been encouraged along that path by

11

institutions such as the World Bank and the International Monetary Fund (IMF), which link the provision of loans to conditions relating to structural adjustment. This has meant that financial support and advice has been linked to the implementation of market friendly structural reform in the economy in question.

Despite all the pains of recent years, however, it is likely that developing countries and the former Eastern Bloc will want to continue to move towards liberal capitalism, attracted by Western levels of prosperity and consumption. While the timescales for achieving such targets are uncertain, there seems little doubt that some countries will achieve greatly increased levels of national output and per capita income. But as Carley and Christie (1992) point out, ironically, the drive for economic growth and hunger for Western levels of consumption in the newly industrializing countries and the ex-Communist world are developing precisely at the point at which consumerism in the West is beginning to appear socially self-defeating and ecologically unsustainable.

The enormous expansion of world trade has been a characteristic of the spread of capitalism and fundamental to the internationalization of the industrial system. The central institution which lays out the terms of engagement in the international trade system and which monitors trade is the World Trade Organization (WTO), responsible for management of the General Agreement on Tariffs and Trade (GATT). The Uruguay round of GATT negotiations on removing trade barriers began in 1986 and was completed in 1993. Environmental considerations were largely ignored during this process, reflecting the sad fact that issues of international trade and environmental management are seen as separate and discrete. Indeed, while at the 1992 Rio Summit governments and other agencies made declarations in support of the principles of sustainable development, when involved in the GATT negotiations, they were making decisions which could undermine progress towards sustainability.

GATT has consistently acted in favour of free trade over environmental protection. It has consistently linked environmental issues to the issue of protectionism and has ignored issues of sustainability. In 1991 GATT overruled an American ban on imports of tuna fish from Mexico (claimed to be fished in such a way as to kill an unacceptable number of dolphins) on the grounds that such a restriction would violate free trade. Indeed, the GATT view is that restrictions on trade claimed on environmental grounds would be more likely to be mere excuses for protectionism rather than real attempts to reduce environmental damage. One is tempted to ask: 'Whatever happened to the precautionary principle?'

THE CULTURE OF CONSUMERISM

It is all so easy to put the blame on industry for the bulk of environmental degradation and this book focuses on the strategies which we need to follow to reduce that impact significantly. But we must also examine the reverse side of the coin, which is consumerism. Industrial growth and consumerism are of course, inextricably linked. Consumerism is the vehicle upon which industry can expand, but the promotion of goods by industry also fuels consumerism. At the global level the issues are also intertwined. The industrialized nations are well aware of the problems associated with ozone depletion, global warming and the loss of biodiversity. They know that the economic expansion and growth of developing countries threaten to make the situation worse, but they cannot deny other countries the right to improve living standards from often very low bases. It seems evident that the planet cannot sustain the globalization of a Western consumer lifestyle, but governments are unwilling to accept that there must be a limit to material consumption.

One of the major factors which has allowed consumerism to boom has been the massive advances in technology and technological capability. This has allowed more raw materials to be extracted, and more to be processed and distributed in less time with less labour. That technology has been concentrated in the West, of course. The result has been that the scale of Western consumption compared with that elsewhere is increasingly diverse. According to the United Nations (UNDP, 1992), the 1.25 billion people in the advanced industrialized countries consume vastly more, on all key indicators, than the 3.4 billion who are adequately fed and clothed, and the 1 billion or more who live in absolute poverty. The 5 per cent of the world's population who live in the US consume around one-third of the world's resources.

Although we might argue that history can provide us with all sorts of evidence to suggest that consumerism is not particularly new, a characteristic which we must accept is that the sheer scale of consumption is of a different order from anything known in pre-industrial times or periods of modernity. Mass consumption and the legitimization of individualism (which translates into consumerist attitudes) rather than collectivity is a characteristic of modern society. Society has become increasingly competitive and cooperative, and collectivist attitudes at the level of the local community have been replaced by independent, insular living where money becomes the measure of success and status. Cultural forces are marginalized and notions of local (or even national) self-sufficiency replaced by a reliance on the trade of world commodities produced by an international, industrialized market.

The dominant culture which has been created through the growth of consumerism is now transmitted globally through mass communications technology and networks. In particular, it is the power of advertising and the persuasiveness and pervasiveness of sophisticated marketing strategies which promote a link between well-being, status and consumption. So-called green advertising has its roots in consumerism and has therefore done little to promote environmentalism. Most green advertising campaigns have therefore been cynical attempts to increase market share and profitability without any real regard to the principles of sustainability.

The power of the TNCs is further strengthened through the global images which they are able to present using mass communications technology, including satellite networks and associated broadcasting opportunities. Thus the globalization of the industrial system not only makes the transnational organization increasingly powerful, but it also replaces local culture with an imported, generic, Western-based alternative. There is a gradual erosion, therefore, of local cultural distinctiveness in production and consumption, and a spread in the desire for the imported products which are mostly associated with Western affluence. Such cultural control is hardly compatible with local action, self-determinism and individual empowerment, all of which are needed to move us toward a more sustainable model of economic activity.

Nevertheless, there must be limits to consumerism. Indeed these fall into two types. Firstly, there are the limits to growth imposed by the possible physical exhaustion of many of the world's key resources. But before we ever reach that situation it is more likely that we will see another limit to consumerism and the culture associated with materialistic consumption. This limit will be imposed by social and environmental change. Ecological imbalance, environmental degradation, the growth in the number of major environmental disasters and the breakdown of aspects of social order are all a function of overproduction, overconsumption and associated inequalities between the rich and the poor.

According to commentators such as Durning (1991) there is little correlation between high levels of consumption and personal happiness. Indeed Hirsch (1977) argues that there is something fundamentally self-defeating in modern consumption patterns. He notes the widespread dissatisfaction that accompanies the pursuit of affluence. His argument is that individuals only get satisfaction out of affluence by owning 'positional goods' which remain scarce. But the growth in wealth and the increased availability of goods means that positional goods, over time, become less valued. Therefore the individual in the pursuit of happiness via materialism is constantly disappointed and continually has to find and pay for the next new purchase. The debate which surrounds whether or not consumption equates with happiness and satisfaction is, however, of far less importance than the issue of consumption and sustainability.

It has already been argued that there must be clear limits to consumption, and a growth in consumerism must therefore be incompatible with sustainable development. The challenge is therefore to translate this fact into policies that are able to correct the situation. To date there has been very little thought about this process except by those neoclassical economists who see the answer as internalizing the social and environmental costs of consumption into the prices paid for consuming goods. The emphasis, therefore, has been put on calculating the full costs of externalities such as environmental damage and including these in the prices paid by consumers. The 'polluter pays' principle which establishes the foundation of much environmental policy is an attempt to undertake such an exercise. There are nevertheless certain problems with that sort of approach. Firstly, it assumes that we can accurately assess these additional costs. But all such analyses are open to large margins of error and often come down to personal judgements about the value of an asset or artefact to an undefined population. Secondly, for the cost internalization approach to be fully effective, compensation must be paid for the use, for example, of an environmental asset. This requires that property rights are clearly defined, but for so many environmental goods (eg the air and the deep seas) no such property rights exist. Thirdly, such a full-cost accounting methodology relies on deciding what should be included as an important cost and therefore internalized, and what should be excluded and ignored. While we might all agree that direct pollution from the production of a good should be internalized, the question remains about issues which may be less direct, such as the impact on indigenous populations of developing countries who mine raw materials, the animals which may be displaced from the natural habitats in such a process, or the families of people who die in road accidents caused in part by an increase in freight traffic. The question relates to where the boundaries are established (which is a social, ethical and practical issue); the answer will differ widely according to basic perceptions of policy-makers.

Perhaps, then, the use of the market mechanism, which is what the 'polluter pays' approach relies on, is not sufficient in itself to control the negative effects of overconsumption. There is clearly a role for the political dimension to play, not only at the national level, however, but also at local and international levels. But here there is inevitable conflict between the aims and objectives of local, national and international politicians. Moreover, there will be inevitable problems surrounding the nature of equity within the Western industrialized countries, and between them and the rest of the world.

One of the first questions to be addressed revolves around how much is enough. Just what should be the limits of consumption and who is to determine these? Such questions inevitably lead to the consideration of equity and equality. Within the Western economies there needs to be a debate over the distribution of income, wealth and opportunity. Between countries the same issue needs to be discussed in the context of much wider disparities. If there is to be a limit put on consumption, we must also ask how the available resources are to be distributed. Simply to continue to allocate goods to those with the greatest number of monetary votes, however, would seem to put the whole system in doubt.

We need to think, therefore, more holistically about the future shape of societies and the organization of the global economy. To impose change through political action via the market mechanism and legislation is only one part of the solution. To tackle overconsumption by tackling demand will be insufficient, and there is a need to tackle supply as well. That means making businesses more aware of their activities and convincing them of the need for radical change in the way they carry out their businesses. The starting point must be to make the modern business enterprise challenge its very reason for being and to encourage, persuade, cajole or force businesses to take an ethical stance. When businesses come to realize that we operate in a no-win game, and that if they carry on operating in simplistic ways in order to maximize profits they will eventually destroy their own markets by destroying the fundamentals of the planet on which we survive, then perhaps they will begin to question their very aims and objectives and return to some fundamental ethical questions. That will take time, but we do not have very much time. Businesses and their owners need to be convinced of the need to act in a proactive way and to strive together towards sustainable development. There is an urgent need for educational programmes to convince companies of that need and to provide them with some of the tools to help them to move towards a sustainable future. This book attempts to make a small contribution to that educational process and to the necessary process of challenging accepted norms and procedures. There is a need for us all to be more creative and imaginative and not to be held back by notions of barriers imposed by 'the real world'. Whose world is it anyway – and whose reality is it?

THE MEANING OF 'GREENING'

The greening of industry is a term much talked about but rather less thought about. It lacks a clear definition and remains troublesomely ambiguous, and although it has become a popular target for academic research it is underdeveloped in terms of theory and is untested along

16

empirical lines. Authors such as Gladwin (1993) argue that for research on industrial greening to be broadly utilizable there is a need to take a more scientific approach. This would involve an adequate description and classification of greening, the generalizability of findings and the predictability of conclusions. But is this not simply asking too much? In the postmodern world we must ask whether such meaning does and can exist. We must consider whether it can ever be possible any more to generalize from specific observations, and in terms of greening we must ask whether it is a single process capable of classification at all. If we are to discuss the meaning of greening, it is not possible to describe and predict accurately. A more useful exercise, therefore, would seem to be to prescribe and define what greening ought to be. Central to this process, we must consider where the concept of greening fits into our ultimate aim of sustainable development.

Let us begin, however, with an overview of what greening seems to mean at the moment, from a number of different perspectives on change. Figure 1.1 provides a crude 'spectrum of greening' which measures change. At one end is superficial change and at the other is fundamental change. Ten different forms of environmental strategy are chosen to reflect stages in the greening of industry along a ten point scale. These strategies are categorized by the basic ideology underpinning them, beginning with a simple reactive ideology and ending with an acceptance of the need to base a new ideology around creativity.

Low down on the spectrum of greening are those firms for whom the greening process is fundamentally about add-on pollution control. Those firms are motivated merely by the need for compliance and see pollution prevention as a necessity which adds to their costs. Such firms and such thinking are not unusual. To many, greening is to be found in the practical, technology-based action which, while often proactive, sees change in stark 'technological fix' terms. For example, a rethinking of processes through design for disassembly, rethinking traditional notions of disposability, toxic reduction through clean technology and an emphasis on energy and waste management are common among such firms. Essentially, however, these are reactive strategies.

More proactive firms are beginning to see a role for assessing, monitoring and acting on their environmental impacts through an environmental auditing methodology. The process of auditing is simply an information-gathering exercise and it requires a commitment to a cycle of improvement at the very least. Those firms benefiting most from the auditing exercise will be those who have introduced integrated environmental management systems which represent a step towards a more holistic view of business strategy.

Those companies which see greening as an activity which goes beyond the processes which take place on a particular site or within

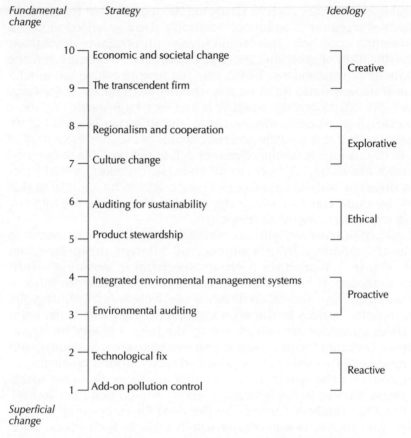

Figure 1.1 *The Spectrum of Greening*

the organization more widely are increasingly committing themselves to product stewardship strategies. Thus they take responsibility for the products they produce from cradle to grave. In other words, they undertake a full lifecycle assessment of their environmental impacts from the extraction of raw materials, through distribution and processing, to sale, use and disposal. Companies embarking on strategies that involve the concept of auditing for sustainability examine the impact of all their products and activities in terms of a wide definition of environmental management which moves us towards sustainability. Thus they not only measure direct environmental impacts but also wider social impacts on, for example, ecosystems, animals and indigenous populations in developing countries. This leads us towards much more ethical ways of doing business.

Ultimately sustainability requires us to change the way we do business. This requires us to think about the very way in which we organize the workplace, the way we treat and respond to workers' needs and the very relationship between the business and the rest of society. The process of greening here must be explorative at two levels. Firstly, we must look towards culture change within the organization to change its behaviour, objectives and outlook. Secondly, we must increasingly recognize the benefits of acting cooperatively rather than competitively in managing environmental improvement and defining sustainable strategies which are effective and accepted at a local level. Thus more fundamental change will alter the internal dimensions of the firm and change its relationship with the world around it through policies based on regional development. The radical change here is a move away from the nationally or transnationally based organization towards regional suppliers that facilitate local purchasing policies and a degree of regional independence.

The most fundamental forms of greening have not really been considered in any detail yet except by deep green ecologists who are still seen as being on the fringes of the environmental discourse. However, new ideas that revolve around radical change require us to be more creative in our thinking. Ultimately, the challenge of sustainable development will require some degree of economic and societal change. Firms as we know them may cease to exist. Where firms do exist, they must transcend all other demands, priorities, norms and objectives and place sustainable development as their number one priority if they want to be compatible with sustainable development in the longer term. No firm is close to that, but it is time to begin thinking about how that may be possible and what that organization may look like.

We must remember, of course, that whatever the extent of greening, it is a necessary but not a sufficient condition for sustainable development. In tandem with the greening of industry, this chapter has pointed towards other areas where action is required. Poverty alleviation, population control, health crises, regional conflicts, inequality, famine and starvation, consumerism, political structures, the power of TNCs and a multitude of other issues, all need to be tackled. This book begins to tackle only one part of the problem – the relationship between sustainable development and the business world. It is hoped nevertheless that it can make a small contribution to the enormous task of moving towards a sustainable future. To do that, however, business strategy must be seen in the context of societal change.

SOCIETAL CHANGE

In any discussion about the socially and environmentally aware enterprise or in relation to the tools of corporate environmental management, the concept of sustainable development is at the forefront. Too often, however, that term is being used by 'corporate environmentalists' to justify an incremental approach to improvement, stressing the environment as a single issue subject (see Welford, 1997, for example). Sustainable development is a radical concept and as such it must be removed from such predictable patterns of interpretation. It is not a concept which lends itself to the piecemeal marginalism which we have seen to date, and as a radical concept it demands more imaginative and creative vehicles to put it into practice. In its radical form (Engel and Engel, 1990), sustainability combines independent development with the concept of regionalism, not dependent development in a globalized world.

One of the challenges of sustainable development is for us to consider modes of industrial organization as well as the internal organization of the firm leading us towards a future which promotes environmental protection and equity. If one starts with the premise that the present structure of capitalism has contributed significantly to environmental degradation and increases inequity and inequality, then our challenge is either to point towards new modes of organization within a post-capitalist structure or to abandon capitalism altogether.

Until recently it was the concept and trends inherent in modernism which defined many of the organizational aspects of both the economy and society as a whole, and individual firms within them. Modernism involved a continuous process of redefining and reshaping of what went before, in pursuit of general principles that were thought to have been desirable for the universal human good (Pepper, 1993). Thus small-scale production was replaced by mass production facilitated through mass communications, so devaluing individuality. Taylorist principles were introduced into the organization, treating workers as simple neoclassical factors of production who are managed by rigid hierarchies. Modernism saw the justification for increased materialism, increased (over)consumption, saturated mass consciousness based on manufactured images, notions of instantaneity, temporariness and disposability. Perhaps even more importantly, it was the vehicle for the introduction of dualist thinking. Such dualism has led to a tendency to separate society and nature – that is, to see them as distinct and opposite.

It is the assertion of this chapter that contemporary writings on environmental management within organizations (most typically business organizations) are based on over-simple, independent categorizations which, in turn, hide the complexities of the environmental debate and the complexities of the individual business organization. Postmodern analysis, on the other hand, requires us to distance ourselves from assumptions of unity and therefore to question the generic codes of conduct which make up contemporary corporate environmental philosophy. It is argued, therefore, that there is no single ideology of universal relevance, and culture becomes divided into discrete spheres. This being the case, we are forced to challenge simple categorizations, structures and codes which purport to move us towards sustainability. Nevertheless, it is argued that within the postmodern context the trend of post-Fordist production allows us to revisit concepts such as regionalism within a contemporary setting.

According to commentators such as Power (1990), postmodernism stands for the 'death of reason' and therefore offers a frontal assault on methodological unity (Hassard and Parker, 1993). It gives validity to all views and perspectives. Through the postmodern method of 'deconstruction' (Derrida, 1978) a whole range of philosophical pillars are brought down. The ambiguity inherent in postmodernism offsets the tendency of commentators to make simple categorizations. Harvey (1989) argues that postmodernism rediscovers the vernacular in architecture, emphasizes the discontinuity in history, the indeterminacy in science and the dignity of all possible perspectives in ethics, politics and culture.

There is therefore a need to move away from the simplistic view of society implicit in corporate environmental strategies, and postmodernism provides us with an approach which describes the world 'out there' more accurately. The 'post' prefix is related to a number of concepts which reflect specific features of a postmodern society. One of the most important of these is the notion of post-Fordism (Piore and Sabel, 1984), which characterizes the business organization in a flexible and dynamic way. A theme associated with the 'post' prefix is that the social and economic structures reproduced since the industrial revolution are now fragmenting into diverse networks often held together by information technology, flexibility and new modes of organization. Hall and Jacques (1989) imply in their work on 'new times' that if we can understand these trends, we should be able to control them. But we should note that this understanding is fundamentally different from the neoclassical economic view which sees organizations as acting and responding in rational economic ways that are capable of modelling and generalization.

What postmodernism also exposes is the nature of empiricism. No matter how scientific it is, the empirical process can never produce an accurate correspondence with reality. Instead, it commonly produces a process of professional self-justification. So-called independent research is limited by the discourses which are already shared within a particular scientific community. The evidence which is produced is, in turn, interpreted and justified within a restricted linguistic domain. As an empirical process starts with its theoretical assumptions intact, data produced through experimentation are defined by reference to an existing theoretical spectrum (Gergen, 1992). Findings produced through empirical science, therefore, do little more than reflect pre-existing intellectual categories.

If one accepts a postmodernist approach, there is a seeming impasse in dealing with environmental issues at the firm level. Indeed, even the notion of sustainable development might be challenged for focusing on a particular model existing within a well-defined theoretical paradigm. However, we ought not to see sustainable development as an end and an aim but as a mode of action which, in turn, has to be addressed in different ways by organizations operating with differing objectives and cultures. Postmodernism therefore indicates that simple procedures which are often embedded in codes of conduct and generic models of environmental improvement at the firm level may be inappropriate.

CONCLUSIONS

According to Steward (1989) the growing green picture is intertwined with a renewal of collectivism, universalism and social purpose. Sustainable development sets the terms for individual and social choice, and green politics represents a pattern of change in which collective identity and universal values assume a new status and significance. The analysis of the new needs to embrace the dynamic of these relationships and not to see any one ideology or cultural form or mode of action as dominant over others. Neither can moral aspirations and direct challenges to current systems and structures (which form the bedrock of capitalism) be consigned to the dustbin of 'naïve, unworkable radicalism'. We need to be imaginative and creative. We need to be forward looking and to accept that present economic and political structures act as a barrier to any improvement which is capable of delivering sustainable development.

The way forward seems to be to combine the collective and the individual, to empower people towards a common purpose with personal choice, and to develop the organization so that it strives towards new imperatives while developing the individual and individuality. This approach stresses the need for new social contracts, for new relationships between owners, managers and workers, and the revisitation of notions of industrial democracy, participation, cooperation and collectivism.

Of course, environmental concerns challenge established political forms. Sustainable development demands both a local and a global approach (based on local action and organization), it demands a reconsideration of equity and a new stress on equality. There are serious limits to the capacity of national sovereignty to deal with the threats to the environment. There may be a need for new national and supranational forums and a recognition of interdependence at the global level (although real action should be at the local or regional level). Moreover, such institutions need also to be more creative and leave aside accepted wisdom and theories maintained by the status quo. The growth of uncertainty and conflict between the 'experts' as to the severity of environmental risk has led to a recognition of the limits of rationality alone and an enhanced status for explicit values (Steward, 1989). Existing structures premised on professional exclusiveness and expert consensus do little but maintain the power of the dominant ideologies. We need to develop further the notions of individual responsibility and collective strategy at the political level and drive these down to the organizational level. The new culture needs to be eclectic and cooperative, individualist and collective.

Green thinking draws on a clear moral stance. It provides a radical challenge which is in our grasp if we are willing to challenge power and reconstruct economic structures in a sustainable way. At the heart of that reconstruction is the need to define and develop new flexible ways of carrying out industrial activity. One of the core values of the green movement is the emphasis on qualitative as opposed to quantitative objectives as a measure of social progress. And this is where the political is synonymous with the personal. Schumacher (1974) reflects the views of many in asserting that when it comes to action we need small units because action is a highly personal affair.

The rest of this book therefore explores in more detail the sorts of business-related strategies which firms will need to adopt to follow a strategy which is consistent with sustainable development. At the very least the whole approach must be based on a sound ethical ideology. Within that context we need to explore contemporary environmental management tools and improve their implementation through a more demanding methodology and a widening of the definition of the environment. We need to explore the role of culture and creativity within the organization. Moreover, ultimately, we need to look towards new modes of industrial organization which (unlike present ones) will be compatible with sustainable development. Because this is a book about sustainable development, it is about the future. Not everything discussed in the book is achievable in the short term, but it is important that we begin the debate now!

Chapter 2

Social and Ethical Issues for
Sustainable Development

INTRODUCTION

The ethical dimension is central to doing business in a way which is consistent with sustainable development. Here it is argued that social and environmental issues are a subset of business ethics and that by considering the structures and procedures which define the ethics of a company we ought to be able to say something about the prospects and preconditions for improvement. Traditionally, business ethics were often seen as a topic which was of little concern to the day-to-day operations of business, where the emphasis was often on maximizing profits without being overtly antisocial. In the 1990s in Western economies and some developing countries a range of stakeholders began to demand greater accountability on the part of business and, more specifically, called for businesses to act in more honest, open and transparent ways.

Nevertheless an emphasis on ethical ways of doing business as a core factor in a business' strategic plans is still unusual. Moreover, the study of ethics is not even that common in the business schools which are supposed to train and educate the managers of the future. Within the social sciences we have seen the study of political economy, for example, replaced by economic science and positive economics, and this has placed an emphasis on theories of optimization rather than sustainability at the firm level. To begin to tackle the challenges of sustainable development we must begin to redress this balance. Western economies have developed along particular paths with an emphasis on industrial growth, efficiency (defined in narrow monetary terms) and performance (usually defined by profits and increases in share prices). The politics of the 1980s that were associated with Thatcherism and Reaganism led to the common cry that 'there is no alternative' and the development of a narrow, profit-centred corporate ethic. In the 1990s a few well-publicized cases of unethical practices led to a number of embarrassments for 'blue chip' companies, but in the new millennium we can expect to see businesses held more and more accountable for their actions. The information society, in which people have increasing access to both 'official' and 'unofficial' information about companies and their activities, will make the internal workings of well known companies much more transparent, and this will mean that they are increasingly unlikely to be able to hide unacceptable practices in the name of profit maximization.

It seems obvious, therefore, that social responsibility and environmental considerations can no longer be ignored in the context of an ethical (and indeed efficient) approach to doing business. Hartley (1993), for example, suggests that the interests of a firm are actually best served by scrupulous attention to the public interest and by seeking a trusting relationship with the various stakeholders with which a firm is involved. In the process, society is also best served because the firm is forced to consider a whole range of competing objectives and to move away from activities which are derived from short-term performance indicators. These various stakeholders which the firm must consider are its customers, suppliers, employees, shareholders, the financial institutions, local communities and government. The stakeholder concept stresses the idea that a company has responsibilities to all these groups (even though they will have unequal amounts of power) and will be involved in balancing the often competing demands put upon it. A company's ethical stance will be influenced therefore both by internal values and by pressures exerted on it from external sources.

DEFINING THE ETHICS OF BUSINESS

The starting point must be to provide a definition of business ethics. This is difficult, because it will depend on both the values of the individuals working in the organization – particularly on the culture created by the individual ethics of senior management – and on any codes of conduct which formally exist within the organization or standards adopted from external agencies. We do not observe one single ethical code in all parts of society, but different codes in different places and at different times, and this is replicated within any business. However, we can distinguish between 'personal value systems' which individuals will bring to the workplace and a 'formal business code' which may exist in some businesses through an explicit set of rules (Burke et al, 1993). Perhaps more importantly, however, we ought to think about the 'actual value system', which is the moral climate experienced by staff in their daily business lives and which determines the behaviour of the firm as a whole, and a 'necessary value system', which is the minimum level of ethics (often equated with legal requirements) which has to exist for the firm to survive.

In a pluralistic society, social, cultural and organizational power structures will tend to interact with these value systems. Such interaction may bring about a consensus or norm in certain areas of business activity, but it may also result in conflict where the ultimate outcome will depend crucially on the balance of power. One of the phenomena we have seen in the last few years is a shift of some of that power towards the consumer and the general public, and this has renewed the interest in business ethics and corporate responsibility.

Another issue which causes problems for those advocating stronger codes of business ethics is that not all desirable ethics are mutually consistent. In those circumstances, judgements have to be made based on valuing different ethical actions. This too is a significant source of conflict. Again though, outcomes will be determined by power structures and dominant ideologies will tend to arise. Such ideologies are nevertheless often a product of compromise and may not necessarily be first-best solutions. This is particularly apparent when we compare the conduct of those companies that are implementing environmental management strategies with the imperatives called for by the concept of sustainable development (Welford, 1993).

The study of business ethics is not new. In the 19th century Utilitarian reformers highlighted the need for ethical principles to be part of the free enterprise system. Currently, the literature on business ethics and on ethics generally is vital and growing. A key issue, however, is that there are many dilemmas where major principles, held to be moral imperatives, can be incompatible in some circumstances. There must exist therefore some sort of hierarchy which places more emphasis on one principle than on another. What we are clearly observing nowadays is the movement of social and environmental considerations up that hierarchy.

Ultimately, however, it is organization which dictates the hierarchy of different principles. The various levels of organization, from whole economic and political systems via institutions and organizations to individual relationships, suggest particular hierarchies of principles (Donaldson, 1989). These hierarchies obviously shift over time and between different economic and political systems. They can be influenced, although that, in turn, will depend on power relationships. Many principles of business ethics might be considered somewhat abstract. A key issue, therefore, is how commonly accepted principles (such as improved environmental performance at the firm level) can be translated into practice. This has to be done via codes (legal and self-regulatory), education, communication and information. But these vehicles for change are themselves open to manipulation by those with power and the best principles are not always translated into best practice. Increasingly, for example, people are agreeing with the principle of sustainable development, but the vehicles for translating that into business practice have stopped far short of real sustainable solutions.

Because language is the basis of communication, it plays a crucial part in the translation of a principle into practice. Commonly, one person's technical term is another person's jargon. Again, the whole concept of sustainable development has come to mean a number of different things to different people. Terms such as sustainability, sustainable growth, sustained growth, sustainable development and sustaining organizations have become confused. Commonly they are associated with environmentalism, and key concepts such as social responsibility, equity and futurity are sidelined. Moreover, when ethical outcomes are discussed, words such as moral, ethical, good, efficient, rational, effective, fair, best and improved, all come to mean different things in different circumstances. The meanings, connotations and overtones of words and phrases are often deployed in the conflicts and struggles for supremacy. The language of management is rich in emotive and ideological content and therefore what companies and managers say they are doing must be treated with healthy scepticism. What they are actually doing, assessed against clearly defined principles and measures, is much more important. Hence in communicating their message about environmental performance, companies must be open and honest and not be tempted along the road of self-gratification and overstatement which we so often observe.

According to Donaldson (1989) there has been a relative neglect of the systematic handling of values in business, which has been self-conscious. The consequences of the neglect can be seen both in anxiety about industrial performance in the West and a rise in concern about moral or ethical issues. A patchy awareness of the problem is to be seen in the sporadic (and at times piecemeal) nature of attempts by governments to regulate industry. This is well illustrated by the uneven growth in environmental legislation in the West and the continued growth of ad hoc codes of conduct in this area.

All organizations operate an ethical code, whether they know it or not. This may not be consistent at all times, but it is based on codes of conduct which are embedded into company culture and through the actions and decisions of senior management. Those codes will also be influenced by society's norms and in the business world by institutions and practices which stress the need to create wealth measured in quantitative financial terms. For any business which wishes to survive or avoid hostile takeover, the system necessarily pushes profits to the top of the corporate agenda and pushes other issues, such as social responsibility and environmental protection, down the agenda.

Moreover, there is no business practice, action or statement that cannot have an ethical dimension. Businesses serve a variety of purposes for different stakeholders. Therefore we might argue that as a necessary condition, business activities are justifiable only in so far as they can be shown to meet the legitimate requirements of stakeholders. However, these requirements can be and often are in conflict, and can change over time. In identifying requirements and reconciling them, we have major problems. Moreover, we have suggested that the principles, ideals and moral values upon which stakeholders' requirements are based can be in themselves contradictory. The traditional way of resolving these issues is for the firm to assume primacy over individuals, allowing it to pursue objectives which are dictated by senior management and subject to financial constraints imposed by owners and lenders. Thus firms often adopt their own identity and culture, and often exist outside the democratic framework. But we must realize that business ought to be a means and not an end, and it is a means for satisfying the requirements of all who have a legitimate claim.

It might be argued that any philosophy or course of action that does not take the public interest into consideration is intolerable in today's society (Hartley, 1993). Today's firms face more critical scrutiny from stakeholders and operate in a setting which is becoming more regulatory and litigious. The notion of public trust is also becoming more important. A clear measure of how far we have come towards a more responsive and responsible business climate is indicated by the fact that if a firm violates public trust, it is likely to be surpassed by its competitors who will be eager to please customers by addressing their wants more accurately. Moreover, while the overwhelming majority of business dealings are non-controversial, any abuses increasingly receive considerable publicity, harming the image of business. NGOs are also increasingly powerful in societies where individuals have more access to information. Media such as the Internet provide a relatively cheap means for NGOs to highlight what they might see as the abuses of power of large TNCs, for example. This phenomenon is not restricted to the West, however, and often it operates in developing countries, where NGOs have been successful in embarrassing large firms that have traditionally paid little regard to social and environmental conditions.

In order to remain economically active, firms need to learn from their mistakes or from those of other firms. They need to take care to avoid situations and actions that might harm their relationship with their various stakeholders. In the worst of all cases, where a firm faces a catastrophe suddenly and without warning, its whole market image and business strategy can be destroyed. Examples of such events are increasingly commonplace. For example, in the case of Union Carbide, when one of its chemical plants in Bhopal, India, leaked 40 tons of toxic chemicals, the event had (and still has) a profound effect on the reputation of that company. Although the company quickly rushed aid to the victims, it was bitterly condemned for complacency and the loose controls that permitted the accident to happen in the first place. Other companies such as Shell have had their image tarnished by their activities in places such as Nigeria, and have been forced to reconsider their whole approach to social, environmental and ethical issues.

Environmental considerations are only one of the many issues that might be included under the umbrella of business ethics. It is nevertheless an issue which has grown in importance. As a result of the many accidents and growing environmental damage caused by firms, there have been increasing demands from consumers for firms to operate more ethically in this area. The consumer movement has shaped and contributed fundamentally to the significant increase in legislation and regulation at all levels of government. This has been aimed at preventing abuses in the marketplace and the environment, and therefore environmental management strategies are increasingly commonplace in the leading companies around the world. To date, however, environmental considerations have not been given enough attention within the framework of business ethics because dominant ideologies are being shaped more by short-term financial considerations than by the need to do business in a sustainable way. Increasingly, it is social issues which are also being seen as important to stakeholders and, although even more difficult to define, control and quantify, these issues will be increasingly important to firms that wish to project a positive profile of their activities.

CODES OF CONDUCT AND STANDARDS

Although there has been an increasing amount of regulation covering a range of environmental issues, the European Union's intent within its Fifth Environmental Action Plan has been to put more and more emphasis on market-based and voluntary measures. Coupled with this, deregulation measures, introduced by more right-wing governments to appease industry, have been seen in some European countries and have meant even more emphasis being put on voluntary codes of conduct and standards. Of course, it was industry itself which lobbied for the European ecomanagement and audit scheme to be voluntary when the first draft suggested that it might be mandatory for the worst polluting industries. Codes of conduct such as the International Chamber of Commerce and World Business Council's Charter on Sustainable Development, and standards such as ISO14001, have certainly had a significant impact on the environmental profile and practices of companies, but they too have not been without their critics. They provide a framework for businesses to implement their own systems, plans and targets, but the underlying motivations for adopting such codes and standards are not always so clear and questions have been raised as to whether they go far enough down the road of sustainable development. The design and definition of voluntary codes and standards are therefore important to consider.

Codes of conduct defined within an organization or imported from elsewhere in the form of standards are usually associated with practical sets of rules and guidelines. They tend to be expressions of mixtures of technical, prudential and moral imperatives. They influence behaviour and therefore ethical outcomes. However, standards which are externally driven are typically expressed in a form that is well protected from discussion, expressing aims in a matter-of-fact language (Donaldson, 1989). In turn, therefore, a standard carries with it a dominant ideology which, because it is standardized, has a multiplier effect and increasing weight if the standard becomes a norm.

The adoption of codes of conduct and standards within any organization necessarily raises a number of questions. The most obvious one concerns the type of subculture which a standard brings with it. Does it represent a piecemeal attempt to placate demands from pressure groups and consumers or is it a more serious attempt at ethical behaviour? We ought also to ask how effective the codes are in promoting what they stand for. Taken together, these questions provide a measure of the extent to which the standards are genuine and operational rather than cynical and self-deluding.

Codes of conduct, and particularly standards, which become accepted across firms in an industry or even across industries are very powerful, and we often see them written into contracts between organizations. We might be inclined to think that a standard promoting some sort of environmental improvement is a huge step forward and that companies which follow others in adopting such standards should be congratulated. But rather more analysis of the content and purpose of such a standard is necessary before we can reach an answer to that question. Without suggesting that environmental standards are indeed bad, we must nevertheless consider whether, in fact, some standards push employees and customers into a set of values which verge on indoctrination. Stakeholders in those sorts of situations come to possess what Marxists see as false consciousness. In addition, the fact that a standard is widely accepted does not guarantee that the values within it are not restricted or inconsistent. Values contained in standards can also be restricted when, for example (and typically), they exclude any consideration of the impact of a company's activities on indigenous populations in developing countries.

There is very little research on the generation, operation, monitoring and amendment of codes and standards. However, it is argued forcefully by Donaldson (1989) that because codes tend to be expressions of mixtures of technical, prudential and moral imperatives, and because they tend to vary in the extent to which they are or can be enforced, they cannot be regarded as the major vehicles for identifying and encouraging the practices which will raise the level of values in business and industry. Moreover, codes and standards are defined outside the normal democratic framework which determines laws. They are constructed by agencies (often professional bodies or representatives of senior management in industry) with their own motivations, values and interests. On this subject Donaldson and Waller (1980) point to a statement of Bernard Shaw when he asserted that professions can be conspiracies against the laity; and their codes, it may be added, are widely held to be primarily aimed at the protection of the members of the profession rather than the public. Much the same accusation might be levelled against industrial standards. Moreover, the matter of the development of codes and standards is bound up with the matter of enforcement. Codes which are not enforced or fail to deliver their expected outcomes, for whatever reason, might be thought of as little more than cynical expressions of pious hopes.

Much of what has been discussed here can be illustrated by reference to the Responsible Care Programme, which in itself provides a standard for firms operating in the chemical industry to adopt. The Responsible Care Programme might be seen as one of the earliest environmental management systems standards used across companies. It is a voluntary code where performance is measured in terms of continuous improvement. Responsible Care is unique to the chemical industry and originated in Canada in 1984. Launched in 1989 in the UK by the Chemical Industries Association (CIA), the cornerstone of the system is commitment. Chief executives of member companies are invited to sign a set of guiding principles pledging their company to make health, safety and environmental performance an integral part of overall business policy. Adherence to the principles and objectives of Responsible Care is a condition of membership of the CIA. All employees and company contractors have to be made aware of these principles. The guiding principles also require companies to:

• conform to statutory regulations;
• operate to the best practices of the industry;
• assess the actual and potential health, safety and environmental impacts of their activities and products;
• work closely with the authorities and the community to achieve the required levels of performance;
• be open about activities and give relevant information to interested parties.

A company operating the Responsible Care Programme is required to have a clear company policy and the communication of this is seen as vital. The key principle being used in the Responsible Care Programme is self-assessment. However, the CIA does assess the effectiveness of the programme across all firms by collecting indicators of performance from the firms. Companies are encouraged to submit six classes of data to the association. Individual company data are not published but a national aggregate figure is published annually. This shows industrial trends and enables individual companies to assess their own placing accordingly. The six indicators of performance are:

1 Environmental protection spending
2 Safety and health (lost time, accidents for employees and contractors)
3 Waste and emissions
   – discharges of 'red list' substances
   – waste disposal
   – an environmental index of five key discharges by site
4 Distribution (all incidents)
5 Energy consumption (total on-site)
6 All complaints.

A key element of the Responsible Care system is the sharing of information and participation of employees and the local community. Local Responsible Care 'cells' operate for the exchange of information and experience between firms. Employee involvement is also encouraged and the CIA has established training programmes which set targets for appraisal. Firms are also encouraged to have community liaison groups and initiatives that recognize the continuing need to forge improved relationships with the public.

However, in its three-year report of the Responsible Care Programme (ENDS, 1993) the CIA was forced to admit implicitly that the Responsible Care Programme was not functioning in accordance with its aims. The main reason for this is that sites claiming to adhere to the Responsible Care standard were simply not adhering to its principles. Over the three-year reporting period, only 57 per cent of firms made returns for all three years and only 74 per cent made any returns at all. Even more importantly, the third indicator of performance deals with waste and emissions where firms are supposed to report an environmental index by site, designed to give a composite picture of gaseous, liquid and solid releases. Only one-third of the total firms which were supposed to be operating Responsible Care reported these data in full, and of those which reported the index, over 30 per cent reported a worsening environmental impact.

Codes of conduct are therefore nothing if they are not adhered to and voluntary approaches often slip down a list of priorities when other pressing issues arise. It is perhaps not surprising that the lack of response from the chemical industry over Responsible Care occurred during a particularly bad economic recession. However, at the core of a strategy for environmental improvement there has to be commitment, and no standard or code of conduct will survive without that commitment. While some chemical companies are clearly committed to improving their environmental performance, it seems that too many are not adhering to the spirit of Responsible Care. Indeed, while some make efforts to follow the guidelines of the programme, many more treat Responsible Care as a smokescreen. Many of those managers in the chemical industry who appear confident of their procedures to improve environmental performance are certainly either suffering from the false consciousness which was suggested earlier or are making much more cynical attempts to hide their environmental impact in an attempt to hang on to market share and profitability.

THE CONTRIBUTION OF ETHICS TO SUSTAINABLE DEVELOPMENT STRATEGIES

Ethics refers to standards of proper conduct. Unfortunately, there is often not complete agreement as to what constitutes ethical behaviour. In the case of illegal and exploitative activities, there is not much dispute. But many practices fall into a grey area, where opinions may differ as to what is ethical and what is unethical and unacceptable. Possible examples of environmental strategies which fall into that grey area relate to the ecolabelling of products and claims associated with the environmental friendliness of a product. These are examples of firms using tactics to persuade people to buy, often misleading customers into thinking that they are getting a product which will not harm the environment, and exaggerating advertising claims. Unfortunately, some business firms have decided to 'walk on the edge' of ethical practices (Hartley, 1993). This is a dangerous strategy, because the dividing line will be different for everybody. Moreover, what society once tolerated as acceptable behaviour is rapidly becoming unacceptable and firms which choose to position themselves so close to criticism will end up battling with time. To a large extent business ethics are firmly on the agenda for the new millennium. Society expects, and is now demanding, much more ethical conduct whereas it had previously regarded questionable practices with apathy or ignorance.

It is now no longer justifiable to see business ethics as directly connected with the law and 'necessary value systems' as inappropriate. The relationship between ethical conduct and the law is sometimes confusing. Naïve businesses might rationalize that actions within the law are therefore ethical and perfectly justifiable. But an 'if it's legal, it's ethical' attitude disregards the fact that the law codifies only that part of ethics which society feels so strongly about that it is willing to support it with physical force (Westing, 1968).

Many businesses assume that the more strictly one interprets ethical behaviour, the more profits suffer. Certainly, the muted sales efforts that may result from toning down product claims or refusing to buy raw materials which result in the exploitation of indigenous populations may hurt profits. Yet a strong argument can also be made that scrupulously honest and ethical behaviour is better for business and for profits. Well-satisfied customers tend to bring repeat business and it is therefore desirable to develop trusting relationships with not only customers but also with personnel, suppliers and the other stakeholders with which a firm deals. An unbending disavowal of the unethical practices such as false environmental claims and improper waste management can create, in turn, a healthier business culture for an entire industry. A firm's reputation for honest dealings and environmental action can also be a powerful competitive advantage. Ethical conduct is not incompatible with profitability but it does change timescales. It is more compatible with maximizing profits in the long run, even though in the shorter term disregard of these ethical principles may yield more profits.

Unfortunately, the perception that unethical and shady practices will yield more sales and profits still prevails in many organizations. Given the institutional setting of the modern capitalist economy, there are certain factors which can be identified that tend to motivate those less than desirable practices. These include an overemphasis on short-term performance, the dominance of competition over cooperation, expediency and indifference, and a dominant ideology towards environmental management which stresses piecemeal approaches rather than a strategy based on the principles of sustainable development. Let us examine these issues in more detail.

The overemphasis on short-term performance

In most firms, career development and higher salaries depend on achieving greater sales and profits. This is true not only for individual employees and executives but for departments, divisions and the entire firm. The value that stockholders and investors, creditors and suppliers place on a firm depends to a large extent on growth. In turn, the dominant measure of growth is increasing sales and profits. The better the growth rate, the more money is available for further expansion by investors and creditors at attractive rates. Suppliers and customers are more eager to do business. Top-quality personnel and executives are also more easily attracted.

In particular, the dominant drive would seem to be towards profits and profit maximization. This is justified by economists such as Friedman (1963), who argues that 'few trends could so thoroughly undermine the very foundations of our free society as the acceptance by corporate officials of social responsibility other than to make as much money for their stockholders as possible' (p133). Friedman's view, and that of many others, simply neglects the responsibility that all actors in society have to benefit society in terms which are wider than the narrowly based performance measures which he adopts.

The emphasis on quantitative measures of performance and on growth, in particular, has some potential negative consequences. In particular, it tends to push social and environmental issues down the corporate agenda. If growth can be achieved at the expense of marginal environmental damage, then little account will be taken of the real impact of this damage. The emphasis on growth becomes all pervading and environmental objectives (which may or may not exist) are compromised. Even where the objective is to maximize growth subject to other constraints, growth can easily be justified by devaluing the importance of those other constraints. Moreover, with a dominant growth strategy, people are not measured on the basis of their moral contribution to the business enterprise. Hence, they become caught up in a system which is characterized by an ethic which is foreign to and often lower than the ethics of human beings (Holloway and Hancock, 1968). That tends to devalue the role of the worker and of those involved further down the supply chain. It is little wonder, therefore, that when it comes to the consideration of the effect that the production and processing of raw materials might have on indigenous populations in developing countries very little weight is attached to the needs and aspirations of these peoples.

The dominance of competition over cooperation

An intensely competitive environment, especially if coupled with a firm's inability to differentiate products substantially or to cement segments of the market, will tend to motivate unethical behaviour (Hartley, 1993). The actions of one or a few firms in a fiercely competitive industry may generate a follow-the-leader situation, requiring the more ethical competitors to choose lower profits or lower ethics. Moreover, in a fiercely competitive environment the objective of the firm is dominated by the need to increase market share, to stay one step ahead of competitors and therefore to adopt isolationist and independent strategies. To succeed in the marketplace, businesses feel the need to cut costs, to downgrade other objectives which might be perceived as expensive, and to cut corners where possible.

That is not to suggest that competition is bad but that its dominance does mitigate against the opportunities which can be brought about through cooperation. Moreover, environmental issues are often overlooked because they are perceived as adding to costs, with any benefits being somewhat intangible. Cooperative strategies can lead to synergetic benefits to businesses within a region or industry and can prevent the wasteful duplication of resources in many areas (Welford, 1993). Such a strategy leads to the sharing of experiences and the sharing of the costs and benefits of research and development which, in turn, encourages all firms to adopt best practices and procedures.

Expediency and indifference

The attitude of expediency and indifference to the customer's best interests accounts for both complacency and unethical practices. These attitudes, whether permeating an entire firm or affecting only a few individuals, are hardly conducive to repeat business and customer loyalty. They are more prevalent in firms with many small customers and in those firms where repeat business is relatively unimportant. But such attitudes also have an impact on environmental issues. They tend to mean that corners are cut and due care is not taken to protect society and the environment. They tend to increase the unnecessary use of resources and generate excessive waste, and to mitigate against the adoption of systems and procedures that can prevent accidents and environmental damage. Moreover, indifference and apathy tend to mitigate against accepting the responsibility which every individual and every firm has in protecting the environment now and into the future.

The dominant ideology towards environmental management

Significant evidence exists that management trends which become popular exert a strong influence on the on-going techniques of corporate management. New concepts which are successfully implemented in certain organizations become accepted, dominant and, even when they are inappropriate, the norm (Mintzberg, 1979). DiMaggio and Powell (1983) offer three explanations for this phenomenon. Firstly, organizations will submit to both formal and informal pressures from other organizations upon which they depend. Secondly, when faced with uncertainty, organizations may model themselves on organizations that have seemed to be successful and adopt the sorts of techniques which they see being introduced. Thirdly, normative pressures which stem from a degree of professionalism among management can cause the adoption of 'fashionable' management techniques. Universities, training institutions, standard-setters and professional associations are all vehicles for the development of these normative rules.

These are precisely the trends we are seeing in contemporary approaches to environmental management, which are often piecemeal and sporadic. This approach is not consistent with the concept of sustainable development because it does not go far enough in developing strategies which will reverse the trend towards environmental degradation. But the piecemeal approach is becoming the accepted ideology because it is being adopted by leading firms, espoused by academics and legitimized by standard-setters and policy-makers.

Moreover, this trend is further reinforced by so-called benchmarking analysis, which is becoming increasingly common in industry. As a principle, benchmarking can be valuable, but it can also reinforce inappropriate general techniques. Current environmental standards are not high, and this in turn gives the impression to imitators in industry that the social and environmental challenge facing industry is actually quite weak. The reverse is true and what is needed therefore is a change in the dominant ideology.

Such a change in ideology is difficult to achieve, of course, because management standards have been set by industry itself. They have been designed to be voluntary and not to conflict with the ideology associated with profit maximization in the short to medium term. Arguments such as the ones outlined above, suggesting that industry has not gone far enough, will therefore be treated with derision by industry and sidelined. The power which industry has in the current economic system is therefore a barrier to further development of the concepts of sustainable development. Thus the only way to bring about a change in this suboptimal dominant ideology is to challenge the very basis of that power. Without a fundamental revolution in the way we organize our society, such a challenge can only come about through a legislative process.

THE PERVASIVENESS OF SENIOR MANAGEMENT ETHICS

The attitudes, values and actions of senior management will tend to form the culture in any organization. In particular, the chief executive will tend to be very important in influencing the behaviour of the next tier of executives and down the line to the shopfloor employees. We know that senior management will tend to have a contagious influence and too often they will have a vested interest that is more associated with short-term performance than in acting ethically. Acting ethically and in an environmentally responsible manner therefore often requires culture change from the top down, but if the chief executive is not keen to drive such change then we must ask ourselves who will.

Related to the top executive's influence over a company is the often mechanistic management systems and structures which so often exist in the most inflexible organizations. These are in place because they are easy to control, but such structures will often stifle creativity. Moreover, any discussion relating to values will be secondary to structure and this will too often define the firm's immediate interests in terms of short-term performance. Customer and employee safety, integrity and environmental protection will be secondary considerations.

While senior management itself may not be directly involved in unethical practices, it often promotes such behaviour by strongly insisting on short-term profit maximization and performance goals. When these goals are difficult to achieve and not achieving them can be met with severe penalties, the climate is set for undesirable conduct: deceptive advertising, overselling, adulterated products, inappropriate waste-management practices, negligence towards environmental standards and other unethical behaviour. A clear alternative to the mechanistic, management-dominated approach is to encourage the participation and creativity of the workforce and make them feel valued. This, in turn, encourages commitment to the organization, better work practices and avoids the problems associated with apathy and indifference (Welford, 1992).

STRUCTURAL BARRIERS TO ETHICAL BUSINESS AND ENVIRONMENTAL MANAGEMENT

The very nature of the contemporary capitalist structure which stresses competition, the maximization of profits and the reduction of costs acts as a fundamental barrier to the adoption of ethical practices in business. In many markets, particularly where oligopolistic structures exist, we often see strategies which are based on tacit collusion where firms will follow dominant market leaders. It is often perceived that unless such a strategy is adopted, firms will be at a competitive disadvantage and their viability may even be threatened. Therefore what becomes accepted business practice by dominant firms tends to permeate a whole industry so that the dominant ideologies associated with the most profitable companies perpetuate themselves and set the tone for business strategies. In these circumstances it is market share and financial performance which come to dominate other measures of the success of the company.

On the other hand, in times when demand falls or when any firm finds itself in a very competitive situation, financial indicators remain dominant and cost-cutting often prevails. However, we know that in two major catastrophes, Bhopal and the Alaskan oil spill, cost-cutting severely affected safety measures and contributed greatly to the gravity of the problem and the consequent handling of it (Hartley, 1993). Whatever the market structure, therefore, success is measured first and foremost on principles of financial management and wider ethical considerations are sidelined. The overemphasis on money, dictated by the economic system, therefore represents a barrier to the adoption of sustainable environmental strategies.

According to Donaldson (1989), however, the most serious barriers to improvement are not in the nature of people or business and industry, but are attitudinal. There is, therefore, a need to change attitudes via a change in the culture of an organization. Central here is a commitment towards improved ethics. Many studies have demonstrated the ease with which the commitment of employees can be gained through methods associated with behaviourial science (Luthans, 1985). While such techniques are sometimes criticized as being potentially manipulative, we must recognize that they hold great potential for increasing ethical behaviour. However, we are not seeking a bolt-on morality (so often common with codes of conduct and standards) but a genuine attempt at introducing real ethical improvements.

This inevitably leads us to consider whether current bureaucratic structures in society and industry are conducive to the introduction of systems which promote ethical behaviour. The stunted development of any consideration of alternative forms of bureaucracy provides us with a major challenge for the future. There is a need for more innovation and imagination on the part of management. Cooperative and participative forms of industrial organization, for example, have often been seen as appropriate only to alternative small artisan operations or have been a last-resort attempt at rescuing businesses which are due to close for commercial reasons. Ethical concerns (and particularly environmental concerns) challenge us to look more closely at developments which are associated with industrial democracy and alternative industrial arrangements. The bureaucratic habits of hierarchy and the narrow distribution of power may not be conducive in the end to a sustainable future.

OPERATIONAL BARRIERS TO ETHICAL BUSINESS AND ENVIRONMENTAL MANAGEMENT

Businesses are also prevented from acting in a more environmentally friendly way by ideologies relating to product responsibility, promotional activities and international trade which are based on custom and practice rather than on any real evaluation of ethical considerations. There is an accepted code of conduct in each of these areas which, once again, stresses short-term performance, perceives change as being costly and fundamentally devalues the rights of individual human beings. It is worth examining each of these issues in turn.

Product responsibility

The traditional view of a product is that once it is sold the responsibility for its safe use and disposal passes to the consumer. That cut-off point means that firms often do not consider the environmental damage done by the use and disposal of the product which it produces. More forward-looking companies are now accepting that the product which they produce is fundamentally their responsibility from cradle to grave, and the most advanced companies have introduced product stewardship procedures to ensure that a product is used correctly and disposed of in an environmentally friendly way. However, this approach is yet to be found throughout industry, where the dominant ideology seems to stress the idea that property rights imply responsibility, so that as soon as such rights are transferred through the sale of the product, the company no longer has a duty of care against social and environmental damage.

Promotional activities

Promotional activities are designed to increase sales and are judged on the basis of so doing. The whole experience of green marketing to date has been associated with exaggeration and deception. There is often a temptation in marketing departments to exaggerate a little and to overemphasize a product's attributes. Unfortunately, moderation is not always practised. Mild exaggerations often multiply and become outright deception. With many products, false claims can be recognized by customers, who refuse to rebuy the product. But where such claims cannot be substantiated easily, false claims are harder to detect. Nevertheless pressure groups and competitors are always willing to expose unreasonable claims and that damages not only product sales but also the reputation of the firm. Advertising statements, if well presented and attractive, should induce customers to purchase the product. But if the expectations generated by advertisements are not realized, there will be no repeat business. Repeat business is the very thing most firms seek: a continuity of business, which means loyal and satisfied customers.

International trade

Many firms today do business worldwide and source their raw materials from a range of countries. Although this presents great opportunities, it also poses some problems, some ethical dilemmas and many opportunities for abuse. Unethical practices have a critical effect on the image of companies at home and abroad. Union Carbide's acceptance of lower operating standards in its operations in developing countries led to the Bhopal accident. The lesson to be learned is that standards and controls must be even more rigidly applied in countries where workers and managers may be less competent than they are in more economically and educationally advanced countries. A major ethical question also revolves around the sourcing of raw materials from parts of the world where indigenous populations are adversely affected. The drive for low-cost inputs leads to the exploitation of such people, the abuse of their land, and attacks their fundamental rights to lead their lives as they would wish.

MOVING TOWARDS SUSTAINABLE DEVELOPMENT THROUGH INDUSTRIAL DEMOCRACY

It is commonly claimed that there is an inevitable trade-off between profit and ethics or morals and that the ultimate constraint to improved ethical behaviour is the need to show an acceptable rate of return on investment. The counter-claim is that behaving ethically is good business and that taking an honest and ethical approach to industrial activities will lead to satisfied customers and repeat business. There are two problems with each of these arguments. Firstly, they assume implicitly that we can measure ethics and thereby characterize 'the ethical firm', or provide lists of good or bad practices. The notion of the ethical firm is not only difficult to describe but attempting so to do is also fruitless. Secondly, both arguments assume implicitly an underlying business structure where the primary outcome is profitability, even though alternative models might be more applicable.

There is a need to look towards alternative ideas and alternative structures. Many of these actually require marginal changes but can bring about much improved outcomes. For example, key procedures are associated with reforms in the workplace which firms can adopt to push them along the path of more ethical behaviour. This revolves around issues of industrial democracy and respecting the values of everybody associated with a firm or organization. More open procedures and less hierarchical bureaucracy in decision-making could be developed within firms. This in turn needs to be linked to an ethical awareness-raising campaign both within and external to the firm, helping to raise the overall ethical profile.

The debate surrounding bureaucracy is too wide to discuss here. But one of the most important points, which is of direct relevance to the contemporary business scenario, is expounded by Argyris (1964), who argues that firms typically place individuals in positions of passivity and dependency that are at odds with the needs of mature individuals. Bennis (1972) and Burns and Stalker (1963) go further in suggesting that bureaucracies are too inflexible to be able to adapt to changes in increasingly volatile and discriminating markets. Traditional bureaucracies reserve decision-making to the top of the organization and decisions are subsequently handed down. Because of the narrow constituency involved in the decision-making process, they may not only be suboptimal decisions but may be severely at odds with the values of a workforce. Bureaucracies hold within themselves methods of controlling and channelling information. Those with power in the bureaucracy will go to great lengths to ensure conformity to internal codes and they have a great range of sanctions available to them for persuasion and enforcement. We have already argued that such codes may be at odds with more ethical behaviour. Flatter hierarchies, participative decision-making and increased self-determination by workers seem to be obvious initial steps to be taken to begin to resolve such problems. We will return to this assertion throughout the book.

If increased industrial democracy better enables firms to act in ethical ways and if the many advocates of participative arrangements (eg Welford, 1989) are right in suggesting that participation improves productivity and performance, then we need to consider why we have not seen manifestations of this form of industrial organization. Any movement towards some form of corporate democracy is taking place slowly and in a piecemeal fashion. But it might be accelerated if legislation which more freely permits different styles of participation and democratic processes was to be introduced, thus doing away with the restrictive structure of authority and responsibility required by law which often inhibits moves in this direction.

CONCLUSIONS

Companies are faced with the challenge of integrating considerations based on the key concept of sustainable development into their production and marketing plans. There is always an incentive, however, for profit-maximizing firms seeking short-term rewards to opt out of their ethical obligations towards environmental management. What is required, therefore, is a thorough re-examination of business ethics within any organization and a change in ideology towards an acceptance by industry of its ethical and social responsibilities. Increasingly in a society where there is easy access to information about the activities of business and a greater willingness to boycott the products of some businesses, managers will realize that an ethical stance is not only important, it will also make good business sense.

Perhaps one of the most important lessons which firms are beginning to learn relates to the desirability of seeking an honest and trusting relationship with customers (as well as with their other stakeholders). Such an ethical relationship requires a widely defined concern for customer satisfaction and fair dealings. Objectives should be written in ethical terms and stress loyalty and repeat business. Such a philosophy and attitude must permeate an organization. It can easily be short-circuited if a general climate of opportunism and severe financial performance pressure should prevail. Indeed, ethical stances to the wide range of issues facing businesses will be imperative if our objective is to move towards a situation which is consistent with sustainable development.

An honest and trusting relationship should not be sought with consumers or final users alone. It should characterize the relationship between sales representatives and their clients, which suggests no exaggeration or misrepresentation, greater efforts at understanding customers' needs and better servicing. It may even mean forgoing a sales opportunity when a customer's best interest may be served better by another product or at another time. The trusting relationship suggests repudiating any adversarial stance with employees, suppliers and, beyond this, with all the communities in which a firm does business. Firms need to throw away ideologies based on financial performance alone and consider their corporate relationship with society. Such a relationship requires sound ethical conduct. It should foster a good reputation and public image.

It has been argued that the competitive nature of markets is often a barrier to corporate environmental performance and creates isolationist strategies. Unethical and unilateral actions may result in an initial competitive advantage but may hurt a firm's overall image and reputation in the longer term. To have a coherent environmental strategy, firms need a consistent set of business ethics and need to measure their performance using a range of longer-term indicators. Placing environmental management within the framework of business ethics also reminds us that it is really not possible to separate broad social and environmental considerations from other more specific issues such as the treatment of women and minority groups, the treatment of animals and the protection of indigenous populations. A set of ethics alone will not necessarily lead to better business practices, however. What we also require is a fundamental re-examination of dominant ideologies in the business world and culture change which is capable of challenging accepted wisdoms.

The rise of organized pressure and interest groups makes it doubly important that managers consider the arguments of all stakeholders in a decision's outcome. Since these groups publicly promote their causes in a single-minded way and do not therefore face the competing objectives so often faced by management, they have an advantage over the traditional company in the strong message which they can convey. Decisions taken in isolation by an élite group are therefore far more likely to result in suboptimal outcomes.

The main thrust of the argument in this chapter, however, is that the major issues and arguments surrounding business ethics, and environmental considerations in particular, are not so much substantive but more associated with procedures and received 'wisdom' associated with structures and hierarchies. It has been argued that these barriers to improved ethics can be removed through the removal of such traditional structures. There needs to be a new emphasis on stakeholder accountability and a move towards new democratic forms of organization within the workplace. There is nothing in the nature of people or of businesses which makes adjustment towards ethical behaviour impossible. Vested interests held by those in power does have to be addressed though, and this is one of the major challenges which we must overcome.

Chapter 3

International Business, Globalization and Development

INTRODUCTION

There can now be little doubt that the environmental damage caused to the planet over the last few decades has reached a point where it is causing untold damage to humans and other species. Much of that damage is irreversible and the massive use of non-renewable resources has taken little account of the needs of future generations. The situation is getting worse, impacting on human health, biodiversity and the social infrastructure of many societies. There is now clear evidence of climate change and we are losing the areas of wilderness left on the planet at an alarming rate. Governments have demonstrated little real effort directed at reversing these trends, preferring to leave the task to the voluntary efforts of businesses, pressure groups, other non-governmental organizations and individuals. Perhaps more than anywhere, the environmental crisis is most acute in the developing world, where it is directly impacting upon the lives and health of local populations. Moreover, environmental crises are directly linked to many of the social problems which we now observe.

Business has to accept a very large share of the responsibility for the crisis. Businesses are central to a system of production and consumption which is destroying life on earth, and if we continue on this path not one area of wilderness, indigenous culture, endangered species or uncontaminated water supply will survive the global market economy. The often uncritical acceptance of trends towards globalization and the emphasis on the need for (naïve measures of) economic growth make the situation worse. If trends towards globalization mean that production shifts to low-wage economies where labour is continually under pressure to produce more at lower costs, then this is hardly consistent with development. In parallel, if growth in the West simply results in underdevelopment in the developing countries, then this simply widens the inequities which are inconsistent with a move towards sustainable development.

Given the current international economic order, what is likely is that the future environmental crises, which are inevitable, will occur not in those countries at the root of the industrialization process, but in those countries which are currently growing at the fastest rates, where business activity is expanding rapidly and where institutional structures are least able to deal with the consequences of accelerating production and consumption. These are the developing countries which have long been neglected in the debates over the appropriateness of corporate environmental management strategies and tools.

This chapter seeks to consider conflicts between sustainable development, the current international economic order and contemporary corporate environmentalism. It does so in four parts. We begin by examining trends of free international trade and globalization. The next section considers current corporate environmentalism in the context of modernism. We then consider changes at the firm level which would be more consistent with a move towards sustainable development. Finally, we return to the macro issue and examine policy changes which would both make the international economic order more consistent with sustainable development and, at the same time, encourage firms to put in place the sorts of firm-level strategies advocated here.

THE INTERNATIONAL ECONOMIC ORDER

In line with the move towards the globalized, free market economy, governments have created an international environment of deregulation, because free markets unrestrained by governments are supposed to result in higher economic growth as measured by gross national output. The primary responsibility of industrial policy seems to be to provide an infrastructure which will help corporations to expand their commercial activities. In this respect, governments seek to enforce the rule of law with respect to property rights and contracts – without which the capitalist system comes to a halt. Privatization has been espoused over the last 15 years and we have seen valuable national assets shifted from the control of governments to the private sector in the name of efficiency. Thus the very role of governments has been to transfer more and more power into the corporate private sector.

Around the world, governments and intergovernmental agencies have shifted towards the more conservative view of economics and industry. The left talks of the stakeholder society and no longer of vested interests and the living standards of the working classes. They now embrace social democratic principles and democratic capitalism. But in general, mainstream political parties have not embraced green ideas. They have operated on the edges of the environmental debate, waiting to see if the green vote will be significant enough for them to respond. They have consistently lacked any real leadership on environmental issues, therefore, and their policies have been devoid of any radical green ideas or vision. The green political agenda (weak as it is) now represents a tension between pressure groups, indigenous protesters and human rights activists on the one hand, and on the other, the vested interests of the large corporations seeking out cheap labour and plentiful resources. This is a battleground where politicians have consistently feared to tread. The resulting outcome is that the more powerful business world is allowed to continue its march oblivious to burning rainforests, rare habitats, dangerous waste sites, unsustainable consumption patterns, the legitimization of greed and ultimately people's lives.

More fundamentally, however, we must now recognize that politicians and governments no longer have sole control over the management of nations. They may still be able to wage war with their massive stocks of destructive arms when opinion polls desert them, but the management of the economic process has to be done in cooperation with business. Of the 100 biggest economic institutions in the world today, about half are countries and half are companies. Only recently have businesses become the major agents in determining how societies and cultures are defined, but they are now expert at it. Indeed, it is business which has created the consumer culture, the fast food culture and insatiable materialism. It is business which would like to set out its vision of the world's monoculture with its global products, global messages and mass markets. It is even business which supports and sponsors the politicians and political parties which will give it what it wants. Money can buy a lot of votes – one way or another. Thus to look to governments for radical change would be tantamount to expecting the big cats to become vegetarian – it isn't in their nature and they wouldn't understand even if you tried to explain.

Moreover, large corporations have a significant advantage over governments. They are able to cross national boundaries much more easily. The TNCs with their massive stock of private capital are much more influential on the global stage than any government or even intergovernmental agency can be. The capital which they use to broker agreements which replace vital natural resources with industrial plant is essentially nomadic. This means that the large corporation is able to change the direction of development of the many countries dependent on its patronage to suit whatever short-term objective seems paramount at any point in time. What development there is in developing countries, for example, is often directed, dependent development and the aspirations of indigenous populations and local environmental concerns are rarely given any real priority. The institutions of government and the intergovernmental agencies which are supposed to protect the greater interest are therefore failing.

There is, therefore, what we might call a 'governance gap'. While we have seen the growth and globalization of business, we have not seen an equivalent globalization of government. There has been no globalization of democracy and virtually no successful initiatives to introduce international regulations governing the behaviour of companies. There is no requirement for companies to be accountable to a global audience, only to be financially accountable in those countries where they decide to declare their profits. This represents a fundamental problem where the power of corporate élites far exceeds the power of any democratically elected institution. In many ways corporations really do now rule the world.

Moreover, companies are very happy to work with many governments in developing countries and often give a good degree of support to them, even where they are not elected democratically and their record on human rights is poor. There is a mutual understanding between such governments and business, and the bottom line is to support each other's aspirations. This translates into collusion between governments and businesses to maintain low wages and poor working conditions. It often means the financial support of government élites. And very often it results in corruption of government institutions. Fees are paid to politicians and senior government officials, syphoned out of countries and into secret bank accounts. Undemocratic governments are able to control dissident voices, often with the tacit cooperation of corporations.

Thus, without the necessary institutional controls on business we have seen our once beneficial corporations turned into finance-driven institutions which thrive on market tyranny. They move smoothly across national boundaries, colonizing ever more of the planet's valuable living spaces. They destroy wilderness in the name of progress, destroying ecosystems and people's livelihoods. People are displaced, their values ignored and the dominant corporate culture invades traditions, beliefs and long-established ritual. The large corporation, the transnational business, is detached from place. It wanders around the world picking off smaller enterprises and influencing sovereign democratic processes. But even productive business is itself threatened by the globalized financial system which it helped to create. This system is less interested in the production of real wealth through productive innovation and more interested in the extraction of money. Thus, as Korten (1995) points out:

> *The big winners are the corporate raiders who strip sound companies of their assets for short-term gain and the speculators who capitalize on market volatility to extract a private tax from those who are engaged in productive work and investment.*

The message here is not one of despair, although it is depressing. It is within our means, however, to reclaim the power that we have yielded to the institutions of money and to re-create societies that nurture cultural and biological diversity. There are huge opportunities for developing social, intellectual, spiritual and ecological advancement beyond our present imagination. But first we must challenge the existing order.

Business so often begins with the premise that globalization is here, it is a reality and there is nothing you can do to stop the trend – end of story. In taking that line it cleverly sidesteps any debate over the inherent contradictions between globalization and sustainable development. While ignoring that debate, it seems content to see the full effects of globalization resulting in a global shift of business out of high wage economies and towards low wage economies. And business itself, constrained as it is by its dependence on growth and globalization, might result in being a major barrier to sustainable development. Here, therefore, we outline three sets of contradictions: between the international economic order (including trends towards globalization) and sustainable development; between the international economic order and business; and between business and sustainable development. Let us deal with each one in turn.

Business and the international economic order

We have seen that in some ways businesses are constrained by the pressure which globalization exerts upon them. The need to make profits in a highly competitive international marketplace means that costs have to be driven down continually. There is little room in corporate budgets for anything which is not perceived as strictly necessary or for anything which does not have a short payback period in a traditional business sense. Such intense competition drives out any scope for creativity, reflection and responsibility. For many Northern companies, simply surviving and maintaining employment in such a hostile environment is difficult enough.

As if to make the situation worse, competitors in low wage economies with access to Northern markets are able to undercut domestic firms. Low wages become a major source of competitive advantage and therefore high wages (as paid to workers in the North) become a source of inefficiency. Job cuts are made or the company itself relocates to low wage economies. Human beings become little more than factors of production, and when the globalized system makes them inefficient they are simply substituted out of production.

The emphasis on cost reduction as a source of competitiveness often, therefore, turns out to be destructive. Moreover, even when companies switch to producing in low wage economies, that is not the end of the potential for cost reduction. The exploitation of the natural environment follows, with firms clearing forests, mining in unsustainable ways and convincing governments to let them have access to more and more resources in order to aid development. Social and environmental responsibility comes pretty low down on any such business agenda. And when breaches of any such responsibility are easy to hide (as they commonly are in developing countries) it does not even focus at all.

The international economic order and sustainable development

The bottom line here is that growth and development are different things. In some cases a degree of growth has benefited development. However, the type of growth we are now witnessing, brought about by the international economic order, is often not consistent with growth. Since development is about a qualitative improvement in the lives of human beings, it is difficult to see how low wage economies, the destruction of natural resources and the undemocratic political power of corporations is consistent with such development. Moreover, economic growth in one part of the world actually requires a degree of underdevelopment in other parts of the world in order to provide the cheap labour and resources to fuel competitiveness. Thus the international economic order becomes divisive and stimulates as much underdevelopment as it creates growth.

Moreover, what development there is is often not sustainable either economically or environmentally. It is too often based on treating the environment as a free good and tends to result in high levels of pollution. It relies on easy access to resources. But such factors cannot last for ever and there is an inevitability about economic collapse following environmental collapse. The future could as easily be about resource wars as it is about some harmonious free enterprise global economy.

The whole process of globalization means that trade in goods and service, capital and labour are free to move around the world as necessary. This greatly reduces the ability of individual firms to put in place policy instruments and other measures which are consistent with sustainable development. The introduction of environmental regulation or taxation could lead to a degree of (perceived) uncompetitiveness and result in less favoured treatment by powerful transnationals. Thus there is a power vacuum and national communities are weakened and are simply not able to respond to sustainable development. Indeed, the international economic order with the support of multilateral financial agencies and the World Bank takes developing countries in completely the wrong direction. As Herman Daly (1996, p157) points out, 'free trade, specialisation and global integration means that nations are no longer free not to trade ... [Yet] this will result in a serious fight, along with class conflicts within nations'.

Business and sustainable development

Clearly the constraints discussed above mean that business actually has a very hard task if it wants to internalize policies and strategies which were consistent with the move towards more sustainable development. However, the nature of business behaviour makes the situation even worse. Since firms seek to maximize profits (even though much of those profits are consumed inside the firm rather than distributed to shareholders), there will always be an incentive for such firms to externalize costs. In the West there are many social and environmental costs which are imposed on companies: minimum wages, national insurance contributions, welfare programmes, health and safety measures, pollution control, liability for accidents, etc. Many of these social costs can be externalized simply by a shift of location. Indeed, what globalization creates is a process of standards-lowering which companies are happy to go along with. They actually create a situation where policies which could move us towards sustainable development, but which would result in costs being imposed on business, are not possible.

Instead, business espouses the voluntary approach where we are supposed to sit back and trust business to move to a situation which is more consistent with sustainable development. Neither will business take the sorts of measures that are required (preferring to create their own discourse on environmental issues, discussed below), nor do most people actually trust big business any more. There is little evidence that much of business is interested in sustainable development, but unfortunately there is a great deal of evidence that businesses are involved in human rights violations, illegal payments to governments, corruption and negligence over pollution controls. But they are now so powerful that there is little that anyone can do about it.

Business has yet to realize that if the international economic order continues and that if the demands of sustainable development are ignored, then they are bringing about their own demise. There is an environmental crisis in the world, but perhaps it is not yet of the magnitude which will force business (and governments) to face up to their real responsibilities. The problem is that when business eventually acknowledges its true role, it may be too late. Until then, it will continue to push a modernist agenda, which we now consider.

MODERNISM AND ECOMODERNISM

The free market, global economic system and its consequential unsustainable path are founded on the vestiges of modernism. Modernism originally referred to the new civilization which developed in Europe and North America over the last several centuries and was fully evident by the early 20th century. But the models of economic development which developed there have come to permeate the whole world along with the Western cultural domination which is inevitable in such a process. Modernism therefore saw new machine technologies and modes of industrial production that have led to an unprecedented rise in material living standards in the North, but which have often resulted in exploitation in the South. The continuation of this process with an emphasis on output growth is what has become so unsustainable. This modernist tradition is therefore characterized by capitalism, a largely secular culture, liberal democracy, individualism, rationalism and humanism (Cahoone, 1996) which are now spreading rapidly to parts of the developing world. As a package, the modern Western model, dominated by technology, science, industry, free trade, neoclassical economics and a fixation with growth, is certainly unique in human history. The results are easy to see: environmental destruction, anthropocentrism, the dissolution of community, the loss of individuality and diversity, the rise of alienation and the demise of tradition. Even notions of development are now often equated only with economic growth. As Shiva and Bandyopadhyay (1989) point out:

> The ideology of the dominant pattern of development derives its driving force from a linear theory of progress, from a vision of historical evolution created in eighteenth- and nineteenth-century Western Europe and universalized throughout the world, especially in the post-war development decades. The linearity of history, pre-

> *supposed in this theory of progress, created an ideology of development that equated development with economic growth, economic growth with expansion of the market economy, modernism with consumerism, and non-market economies with backwardness.*

Modernism, the continuation of what exists, translates into 'business as usual'. Such business practices fail to recognize that the future will have to be very different if we are to avoid environmental and social conflict. Business seems content to see the natural system on the planet disintegrating, people starving and social structures falling apart. Business is powerful in the modern world and must be seen as both central to the problem and central to the solution. If we are to avoid further environmental and social crises, there is no alternative but to change the way in which businesses and markets allocate resources. But that very system, at present, rewards those businesses which can produce goods at the lowest possible capital and labour costs, while largely ignoring the value of nature and environmental degradation. There must be change, and many businesses would agree with that. The conflict is over the degree of change. To date, most businesses which have begun to respond to environmental issues have done so in quite piecemeal and marginal ways. In the developing world most businesses have done even less (often nothing). Thus, as globalization produces a shift of the manufacturing sector towards low wage economies, the process actually makes the environmental situation worse.

Business leaders are not stupid people; they are aware of what is happening in the world around them and often recognize the need for action. They are simply not sure of what to do and often feel constrained in doing anything very positive by the international economic order which requires them to drive down their costs continually. Thus, business currently stands at the edge of a precipice, unsure about which way to turn. Its instincts tell it to stand fast and resist the risky path ahead. But it also recognizes that there is no turning back. Inevitably it is faced with an uncertain future and knows deep down that it will have to move forward into the unknown. At the moment, however, it is hedging its bets by moving forward in minute steps, groping in the dark and doing everything it can to dictate the road ahead.

Business recognizes its need to take a lead because it recognizes its new found power in the globalized marketplace, but it must also respond to a marketplace which is highly competitive and a system which overvalues conventional measures of economic growth. It has, therefore, an interest to make sure that its environmental strategies do not conflict with the arguably more important need to make profits.

Thus, as environmental awareness has increased and there have been calls for businesses to respond in a more environmentally responsible way, business has wanted to make sure that the definition of environmental protection and social responsibility is consistent with its other objectives. Deep green politics are not consistent with the other aspirations of business, which will always be put before the environment. The interests of people in developing countries are less important than the needs of shareholders and customers, and in the globalized marketplace the exploitation of workers in the developing world is fully consistent with the need to maintain competitiveness.

Since there is very little analysis of what a business really is and what its place in society is (in terms of social responsibility and politics), so there is very little understanding of what it could become. And change is often resisted by shareholders, managers and others, who are generally satisfied with the performance of their corporations in the context of the current economic system. But in making such an assessment, few seem really to be aware that their own incomes and comfortable lifestyles often perpetuate inequity which we find around the world. Free-market capitalism does little to solve these problems and it is therefore not the great dynamic entity which its proponents espouse, but actually creates a good degree of inertia to change. The single-minded emphasis on profit, efficiency, cost reduction and growth dwarfs issues such as employment, protection of the environment, social responsibility and sustainable development.

Businesses have yet to realize that the continuation of present forms of industrial activity will simply bring about their own demise. After all, what use is profit accumulation when we are living in a decaying world? The wealthy may be able to build large fences around their property and employ security guards to keep the growing disenchanted out, but there is little they can do to clean up the air around them which is causing asthma in their children. Will industry still be happy with its lot when it has suppressed people's immune systems to such a level that they are allergic to its products, or when their operation has become so efficient that there is no one left in work to purchase their output? When will the business world look at itself honestly and recognize that it is time to change?

Business therefore stands at the edge of a massive potential transformation. However, even when business wants to assume more responsibility for its social and environmental performance, it is often constrained by the international economic order, although with their huge power, large corporations can begin, in fact, to challenge that economic order if they really wish to do so. Large corporations must be persuaded, cajoled or even forced to realize that it is in the interests of all human beings to change. However, it seems that most businesses do not recognize the potential crisis surrounding us, and only a minority are currently committed to change or have any view at all about how to do business better. The reality is that most corporations duck and dive, invest in smokescreens, hide behind science and technology and espouse gradualist, marginal solutions to societal pressures.

Business can and will have to be different if we integrate fully the principles of sustainable development into the international economic order. Hawken (1994) reflects the view of many who believe that there is now the potential for a transformation in the role and responsibilities of business. The marginalism of modernism will not be enough, and change will have to be radical and thorough. It may be that business, in the future, will be unrecognizable when it is compared to the commercial institutions of today. That scenario is entirely possible, but it is currently blocked by business itself and the globalized system in which it operates. Increasing the importance which we attach to development issues in the developing world must be a starting point, along with challenging those who try to interpret sustainable development in narrow terms which often ignore the social aspects of that concept. Indeed, even the term 'sustainable development' is often shortened to 'sustainability'. The concept of development becomes an afterthought; or worse, is simply ignored. And the term 'sustainability' itself is often interpreted even more narrowly in terms of only 'environmental sustainability'. There is a need to consider the development side of the issue in greater detail than has so far been the case.

The present international economic order is, of course, itself a vestige of modernism. The ongoing development of capitalism with its emphasis on enterprise and private ownership has separated economics from ecology and created a dominant ideology which sees the monetary side of economics as more important than the real side. An emphasis on growth rather than on development has encouraged the powerful countries (and businesses) of the North to increase their economic power, first through geographical colonialism, followed by a period of dominating trade and more recently by controlling the ownership and movements of capital. Modern business and economics are therefore now based on liberal-productivist models. Moreover, the international economic order supports such models by imposing, for example, economic austerity measures in the South in order to force a development of the free market economy, reduce wages and cut government spending. These sorts of policies, routinely imposed on developing countries and often with disastrous consequences, are inducing not development but planned underdevelopment. The rights of individuals in developing countries become secondary to the whims of the International Monetary Fund (IMF) economists and the power of commerce in such a system. It is true, of course, that commerce has enriched countries and increased material standards of living, but in so doing it has also created powerful individuals, ruling families and a corporate élite. The benefits of trade and globalization which do accrue to developing countries are not well distributed.

Capitalism has also pillaged the natural environment and created a hierarchy of human beings. The globalization process has removed the rights of developing countries to develop in a self-directed manner and has restricted the rights of most indigenous populations. Such trends have provided many business opportunities, which are picked off by Northern enterprises in a typical predatory manner. Of course, not all large corporations are now based in the North. South East Asian transnationals are increasingly powerful, but their business strategies are based on much the same principles. There is now, therefore, a dominant corporate culture which believes that natural resources are there for the taking and that environmental and social problems will be resolved through growth, scientific advancement, technology transfer via private capital flows, free trade and the odd charitable hand-out. It is undeniable that capitalism has been a great wealth creator because it has unlocked the potential to use basic natural resources and process them into valuable material objects. However, it is also undeniable that, because growth has been so rapid, current wealth is being generated by stealing it from future generations. How will future generations continue the process when there are no resources left? Can this be left to the ubiquitous free market system to sort out?

We should not be surprised to see much inertia in businesses. They find the thought of reconstruction of the capitalist system threatening and difficult to comprehend. They actually feel constrained by the globalization process which forces them to cut costs in order to remain competitive. Industry cannot imagine that it can survive in a world of adjustment which may require cutbacks, decentralisation, less rather than more and free trade being replaced by fair trade. The driving force is more and more profit and the accumulation of ever greater stocks of capital. There is an emphasis on maximizing shareholder value, with much less regard to the impact of consequent strategies on other stakeholders. The basic premise turns out to be that the action which yields the greatest financial return to the individual or firm is the one that is most beneficial to society. But we rarely bother to examine just how profits are made or ask if they are justifiable or in the interests of the wider international community which has worked to produce them. There is insufficient debate over the sources of those profits and just how they are attained. Perhaps when profits are declared there should be some sort of transparent statement relating to just how they were derived, from what sources, and what the associated social and environmental impacts are.

Business is driven by the imperative to replicate money, to increase efficiency and to cut costs. This has a consequent impact on labour. Since labour has to be paid, it becomes a resource which is open to cost cutting. Using more labour than is absolutely necessary therefore becomes a source of inefficiency. Thus there is always an incentive to employ fewer people, to pay them less, to shed labour whenever possible and to replace human capital with technological capital. We are moving, therefore, into a world where fewer and fewer people will be involved in the productive process, and where the number of people benefiting from the activities of industry will decline. The redundant now end up as disenfranchised and in the worst cases become the victims of malnutrition and violence. It is difficult to see how social systems can continue to support growing numbers of unemployed people who in many countries become homeless beggars, criminals, drug addicts and residents of refugee camps. It is small wonder that such people have little consideration for the environment when their main priority is feeding themselves and their families. It is not unlikely that social crisis will be the force for change long before we are forced to respond to environmental devastation.

One of the reasons for the existence of unemployment is that labour is uncompetitive when it is compared with capital. This must be the case, because we observe the substitution into capital equipment, new technology and robotics, thus producing more with fewer labour resources and replacing labour. The globalization process opens up a pool of cheap labour so that even where labour is necessary in the production process, businesses have open to them cheaper alternatives if they relocate in low wage economies. The consequence is twofold. Firstly, we observe growing unemployment and part-time employment in the North. Secondly, we experience the global shift of productive resources to the South. Moreover, in order to remain competitive, labour in the South must accept that low wages are unlikely to increase and, if they do, employment will be lost. Thus we see governments in the South and international financial and development institutions tacitly colluding with companies to ensure the continued existence of low wage economies. As a consequence, the growth of large companies actually requires the planned underdevelopment of developing countries. Rather than seeking to improve the quality of life in poorer countries, the hidden agenda is to maintain underdevelopment. Growth in the North has little positive international 'trickle-down' – it relies on the continued exploitation of the South.

A characteristic of the last ten years has been that large companies throughout the world (although dominantly from the North), facing pressure from a number of stakeholders, have actively become involved in the environmental debate. This has been difficult, because industry is firmly wedded to a free market system which treats the environment as a free good, which has caused the environmental crisis in the first place. Industrialists have considered the arguments of traditional environmentalists, but have generally found them threatening or too difficult to operationalize (Welford, 1997). It is not surprising, therefore, that they have sought out a discourse on the environment which fits within their other aims and objectives. Ecomodernism (like modernism itself), therefore, represents not a break with what went before but is a continuation of it. It adds an environmental dimension to the traditional growth path but does not allow that dimension to change the path radically. Perhaps more importantly, the ecomodernist trend has been subtly designed to reinforce the growth trend, emphasize globalization and ignore most of the social dimensions of sustainable development.

Ecomodernism as a philosophy, with ecoefficiency as its flagship tool, represents a response to concern over the environment by those people and institutions who are persuaded by the need for marginal change, rather than something more fundamental or radical. As such, it represents the hijacking of traditional notions of environmentalism (however disparate) which exist within groupings such as ecosocialists, ecoliberals and ecoradicals, and takes us away from, not closer to, a 'greener' future (Welford, 1997). Indeed, rather than impart any new green values, notions of ecomodernism actually destroy the debate among ecologists, complete a spiritual impoverishment and justify the power of private capital. The tool of ecoefficiency sees no alternative to businesses setting the environmental agenda and controlling the greening of growth through the vehicle of technology transfer via private capital.

Accordingly, any model of environmentalism outside ecomodernism would involve a break with business-as-usual and some sort of discontinuous change. It would challenge the pillars of free trade, scientific and technological domination, and the orthodoxy of continuous improvement and economic growth. It is not surprising that alternatives to ecomodernism frighten the corporate establishment and that their response has been to make sure that the type of environmentalism adopted is consistent with their own aspirations.

Ecomodernism is typified by the following paragraphs taken from the original Declaration of the Business Council for Sustainable Development (Schmidheiny, 1992):

> *Economic growth in all parts of the world is essential to improve the livelihoods of the poor, to sustain growing populations, and eventually to stabilize population levels. New technologies will be needed to permit growth while using energy and other resources more efficiently and*

> *producing less pollution. Open and competitive markets, both within and between nations, foster innovation and efficiency and provide opportunities for all to improve their living conditions.*

Thus, ecomodernism's frame of reference is certainly the here and now, working within the present institutional framework. It sees as a main instrument for change the use of private capital as essential and emphasizes the role of the free market. Moreover, ecomodernism is actually defined to satisfy the wider interests of business. Schmidheiny (1992, p99) reflects this when he argues:

> *Companies now have to work with governments to spread environmentally efficient production processes throughout the global business community... This will require significant technological, managerial, and organizational changes, new investments, and new product lines ... it will be increasingly in a company's own interests to develop cleaner products and processes.*

Such views demonstrate that the sterility of ecomodernism is also one of its key characteristics. Its emphasis on positivism and rationality and its conservative nature means that it denies the existence of spiritual dimensions to the debate which are at the heart of deeper green politics. It calls for technological change in a way which assumes that all technology is good and leaves out any mention of the importance of engaging human beings in a move towards sustainable development. Moreover, and very importantly, ecomodernism is wedded to the ideals of maintaining the wealth of the rich (in terms of both individuals and countries). There is a hidden recognition that growth in one area often creates underdevelopment in another, and this seems to be of little consequence to the ecomodernists. The clear implication of this is that there is always something which will have priority over ecological action. Essentially, ecological action becomes an add-on feature of business-as-usual – given emphasis when time and resources allow, or when crisis or public pressure requires a response.

At the centre of ecomodernism we find the search for ecoefficiency. I have never found a very clear definition of what this really means and that in itself reflects the confused and often contradictory thinking of the ecomodernists. The minimalist definition provided by Schmidheiny (1992, p98) suggests that it is simply 'the ratio of resource inputs and waste outputs to final product'. Thus, using the traditional business tools of systems and audits, ecoefficiency essentially works on the trade-off between industrial activity and the environment, continuing to do business-as-usual and adding concern for the environment. This definition is technologically oriented and implies that solutions can be found which will allow the rich North to consume more and more while using fewer and fewer natural resources. But if managerial science and technology can deliver this ubiquitous 'win–win' situation, there is no consideration of the consequences that this will have on employment and unemployment.

Therefore, we can see that there is a great deal of overlap between models of ecoefficiency and the technological-fix school of thought. This is essentially a defensive school where science and technology are seen as supreme in the defence of traditional notions of capitalism. Industry in the North continues to try to hold on to its domination of the world order by ever increasing its productive capacity through the displacement of labour in favour of capital. This leaves the majority of citizens fighting over an ever-shrinking share of the pie while a small, powerful, industrial élite seek to maintain their vested interests through marginal adaptations to the demands of the rest of us. There is simply no systematic consideration of the full social consequences of allowing this sort of technological determinism. There is no debate over the rights of people and the right to work within whatever economic system exists. This is the world of industrial imperialism.

Those who advocate ecoefficiency talk about 'ecology' when they really mean 'environmental protection' because they do not perceive there to be any difference. Ecologists know that the scale on which we do things is too massive, complex, unwieldy, exploitative and alienating. This is never considered, because the economic system demands greater scale. Mass demand, mass markets, mass consumption and globalization come to dominate any notion of the greening of industry. Even the population explosion is rarely considered because, after all, it does present new market opportunities. Ecoefficiency must fit within the growth paradigm and is actually subtly designed to reinforce it.

The ecomodernist approach sees the future as being a product of what went before. Environmentalism, it asserts, must be embedded, therefore, in what is here and now. The postmodern perspective, which would see the environmental debate more associated with a break from the past, is largely ignored and the usual approach taken to environmental management strategies is therefore largely integrationalist. In other words, corporate environmental management is integrated into (or worse, bolted on to) business as usual. The most significant question therefore revolves around the importance attached to environmentalism. If integration is equivalent to the watering down of environmentalism, it must be seen as a step backwards.

It is increasingly clear that when we discuss environmentalism, many of us are essentially speaking very different languages. The rhetoric surrounding ecomodernism lacks any real vision and ignores the complex social and cultural issues which many of us see as central to sustainable development. It lacks any real dialogue and is largely applicable only to the developed world. Those who want to discuss more radical forms of environmentalism are often ignored and sidelined by businesses. It is asserted by those with power that there is no alternative to the model they have chosen. But they rarely seek the opinions of people as to what they think are the alternatives. They rarely consult powerless indigenous populations in developing countries. Those who demand a greater degree of self-determination and locally oriented development models are told that the world is not like that. The simple fact is that ecomodernism lives with the globalization process, and while others question whether it is always in the interests of development, they are told that they are simply not living in the real world. Is it not strange that such a 'real world' is defined precisely by those people with power who benefit from it? Globalization is never challenged, it is simply treated as a 'given'.

When industry is under pressure, a common strategy is to create forums or clubs among themselves to increase their power further and to provide a justification that they are doing something. One such club is the World Business Council for Sustainable Development, which has been very influential. Established by wealthy businessmen, it has pushed a line which is wholly consistent with ecomodernism. Business clubs are created when public restlessness makes industry feel lonely. Such clubs are essentially fortresses built to fend off the attacking environmentalists. They become a simple mechanism for reinforcing well-established prejudices and ideologies. Well-paid secretariats and project managers lunch themselves around the world in the name of consultation and consensus building. But that 'consensus' is usually well defined a long time before any consultation takes place. Business clubs are therefore very heavy on input but surprisingly light on output. They represent business talking to business and occasionally to governments if they are perceived as being important. There is no attempt to produce a full dialogue with NGOs, people whose lives are damaged by the relentless growth path or the indigenous populations who have their land and livelihoods taken away from them.

One of the problems of the rhetoric surrounding the greening of industry is that it is very repetitive. There are surprisingly few new ideas emerging within business. We simply repeat the same old concepts over and over again, often using different words. We go around in circles rather than move forward towards the real goals of sustainable development. Essentially industry looks backwards; its frame of reference is what went before, and business as usual.

A common characteristic among businesses is only to do as much as they perceive to be absolutely necessary. At the same time, what they do is often given an extraordinarily high profile. For example, it is increasingly common for businesses to draw up an environmental policy. As such, that is a good starting point, but all too often one hears, 'That's our policy, we've got one – it shows we are doing something'. The reality is that too often nothing much happens subsequently. Even those companies which produce environmental reports (and they are sometimes produced for very dubious reasons) still operate as if the environment were an add-on to give them a competitive advantage. Too often any environmental strategy exists outside the day-to-day running of the firm. This add-on rhetoric is dangerous. Those who advocate the addition of environmental protection into business as usual fail to recognize the fundamental faults in the system itself and to deal with the real challenge facing industry: to do business differently.

Many environmentalists recognize the need for action on the demand side when considering the levels of consumption taking place in the North. But the debate in industry always returns to supply side measures because tackling the demand side means challenging issues such as growth and market share, which are sacred tenets to large corporations. Businesses find it almost impossible to conceive of a situation where they are selling less and the emphasis is on ecology and quality rather than on growth and quantity. Increasing populations in developing countries are therefore not viewed as posing severe environmental problems, but perceived as a new market in which to sell goods. The cigarette manufacturers in the North, while worried about litigation, are less worried about falling sales in developed countries when they know that there are millions of people in developing countries who can be targeted in their marketing campaigns.

Managers in the ecomodern firm like simple solutions (and one-page documents) and this is what ecoefficiency offers. They claim that they are busy and need fast, practical and cost-effective solutions to the environmental problem. They fail to recognize, therefore, the enormity of the environmental problem and that there is no single, simple solution to a very complex debate. I find it interesting that seemingly rational managers who claim to care about both the financial and environmental performance of their companies become almost unstable (and often aggressive) when one asks about their social as well as environmental performance. They choose either to ignore their social liabilities deliberately or, more often, are clearly unaware of the social dimension of sustainability and are reluctant to engage in any debate. The ecoefficiency fix therefore rules and actually becomes equated with sustainable development. Social issues are consistently marginalized.

Environmental managers too often seek out only the technical and scientific solutions to their environmental problems. Ecoefficiency actually encourages this and is therefore welcomed. Again, managers are either unaware of the social and cultural dimensions of their activities or are so scared by such ideas that they dare not even consider them. They simply do not know where to start, because they are unaware of the alternatives or are so constrained by a limited corporate culture that they dare not even contemplate anything new.

Because the alternative environmental agenda is diverse and complex and offers no simple solutions, ecomodernists are provided with a stick to beat more radical thinkers. Obstruction through detail is one of the most powerful weapons of the ecomodernists. If one cannot provide them with clear agendas for change, with a detailed (and costed) strategy for implementation, they feel unable to act. They reject alternatives, therefore, with an air of arrogance and a hidden agenda of conservatism. It is difficult to fight against it and cut down the barriers, because the institutionalists are experts when it comes to procedures, protocol and procrastination. What they do not realize, because they lack imagination, creativity and vision, is that the move towards sustainable development is an uncertain path which involves a good degree of groping in the dark.

Uncertainty over other green alternatives therefore only adds weight to the more certain strategy of ecomodernism. It supports the culture of continuity of the past rather than change. In the face of this, the cultural arrogance of some industrialists becomes incredible. They rely on telling us the 'way things are' and 'this is the way things are done around here'. They decry beliefs and feelings because they find them dangerous and threatening. They seek to end the normative discourse through aggressive attacks on anyone who does not fit into their model of the economy and society. The frame of reference of such industrialists is, of course, the continuation of business-as-usual. This is not surprising, since this is where they perceive their own interests to lie. They are willing to take on marginal changes to business-as-usual and therefore tolerate (or even occasionally embrace) ecomodernism, but radical, creative thinking is not on the agenda.

Those who have achieved positions of power and influence often believe that they have done so because they are right and will continue to be right in the opinions which they express. The more powerful they are, the more they simply expect people to listen to and believe their 'wisdom'. Their destructive egos are a major barrier to our moving forward towards a new vision of business.

Finally, we must consider a fundamental question relating to the methodology associated with ecoefficiency itself. If our ultimate aim is to move towards a sustainable development path, we must ask whether the basic concept of efficiency is, in fact, an appropriate measure of sustainable development at all. Efficiency is essentially a neoclassical concept based around optimization, but in the case of the environment we know that to optimize involves an almost impossible trade-off between the many different effects of industrial production. Ecoefficiency turns out to be a complex, messy and inaccurate process which is often related to assumptions about these different environmental effects. When one adds the important social dimension of sustainable development into the ecoefficiency function, then we reach an impossible position to deal with, because it is so complex and uncertain. Such complexity results in businesses leaving the social dimension aside because it would be impossible ever to conceive of a concept associated with social efficiency. Perhaps the concept of efficiency needs to be replaced with the consideration of issues such as ethics, equity, equality, empowerment, education and ecology, but we must recognize that there are no simple models to deal with these issues.

This chapter is not trying to suggest that all the attempts made by industry to improve its environmental performance are bad. It does suggest, however, that to date most attempts are inadequate and that ecomodernism has a life outside other discourses on environmentalism. Moreover, it has been suggested that there are huge barriers to the achievement of even marginal environmental improvements, because of the nature of the international economic order: its emphasis on growth and globalization. Neither the ecomodernist model nor the present structure of the international economic order is consistent with a move towards sustainable development.

Thus I want to paint a picture of considerable concern but not necessarily one of despair. The concern is associated with a view that ecomodernism, although powerful and growing in popularity, might lead to marginal environmental improvements, but lacks the real radicalism needed to bring about sustainable development. We live in a period of rapid change and this is likely to accelerate into the new millennium. Environmental awareness among individuals is exploding, increasing numbers of people are looking towards new solutions to the problems in their lives, and there is a growing distrust of business activity. Industry will have to respond to that change, and although it is now advocating a powerful environmental agenda which is inconsistent with that change, it will have to come to accept the limitations in ecomodernism and embrace the many radical alternatives to that limited discourse. Industry must recognize such change and grasp the opportunities which it presents. That is the focus of the next section of this chapter.

ACHIEVING CHANGE

There are many radical environmental agendas which we could consider here as an alternative to ecomodernism. The work of bioregionalists tells us that it is the scale of industrial production and exchange which is at the root of the problems. Others challenge trends towards globalization and call for a new protectionism. There are those who call for zero growth strategies in the North to allow environmental space for the South to develop. Some continue to hint at the need to replace capitalism with something else, but are usually very vague about what that something else might be. The trouble with all such policy prescription is that it is almost impossible to see such radical change being implemented in the short run. We do live in a global economy and many developing countries and their large corporations are benefiting enormously from their abilities to sell their goods worldwide. Although we know that economic growth is, at times, extremely environmentally damaging, it is nevertheless still the cornerstone of every country's economic policies and seen, in the developing world, as the way to improve standards of living for many millions of people. When one visits countries in South East Asia there is no doubting that this is the case. Thus, although we have argued that there is massive conflict between business, the international economic order and sustainable development, the process of change must start with what is achievable here and now and then build into the more radical dimensions of social and environmental responsibility which are consistent with sustainable development.

It is pointless laying out an alternative strategy which has no hope of being adopted by large corporations which are driven by a desire to gain competitive advantage and growing market shares globally. While many people within such organizations (including senior executives) may be personally committed to environmental improvement, the corporate culture of many large companies in developing countries is such that there is little room for environmental policy unless it can be seen to enhance existing business performance. Thus, everything suggested here is capable of being operationalized in the short run.

We must recognize an important paradox here. This chapter has described ecomodernism as inadequate, partly because it is about supporting marginal change to a business-as-usual philosophy. But it is also being argued that strategies for moving towards sustainable development must be consistent within the aims of the corporation (at least in the short run). This is a paradox, but not necessarily a contradiction. While ecomodernism represents marginal change, here something much more far-reaching is advocated: a new philosophy towards production, consumption and accountability; a recognition of all the facets of sustainable development and how these can be built into a transparent framework; and the recognition that enhanced competitiveness is achievable through differentiation strategies based on social and environmental excellence. This goes far beyond the rhetoric of ecomodernism. While only a start on a long road towards the achievement of sustainable development, it is argued that this agenda is both achievable and superior to the ecomodernist rhetoric.

The challenge therefore is to go beyond the narrow and marginal approaches associated with ecomodernism and to create a degree of change within the constructs of the modern global industrial economy. While it must be accepted that businesses will find this harder to achieve than adopting tools associated with ecoefficiency, nevertheless the benefits of going beyond marginalism may be significant. That is not to suggest that the policies advocated here are cure-alls. They are not. They are policies and tools for businesses in the short term. In the longer term there will have to be a debate about the nature of the international economic order which is at the root of so much unsustainable behaviour.

Here we point towards three areas which ought to be addressed:

- Sustainable production, consumption and accountability.
- Sustainable development at the corporate level.
- Competitive advantage through social and environmental differentiation.

Let us deal with each issue in turn.

Sustainable production, consumption and accountability

One area where corporate environmental management literature is almost silent relates to the definition of sustainable production: a concept which would seem to be important. Here, sustainable production is seen as production which is economically, environmentally and socially responsible. Moreover, 'economically responsible' might be defined as both economic for the producer (ie profitable) and for those involved in the production process (ie in relation to fair wages, employment, etc). Thus a useful definition of sustainable production is as follows: to produce less of higher quality and durability with much lower environmental and social impacts at higher levels of employment, while making an acceptable profit or surplus. The implication is, of course, simple. We should make fewer 'throw-away' goods and more products of quality which will last longer and create less waste. Reuse, recycling and all such associated practices need to be increased. But a fundamental part of sustainable production is to increase levels of employment. Here the argument is simple. If in the search for ever increasing efficiency and lower and lower costs companies continue to use less labour and more capital, then before any environmental crisis causes massive turmoil, social upheaval led by those unemployed who become disenfranchised from society is more likely. We have already noted that labour is becoming more and more uncompetitive as capital productivity increases. But such capital productivity is being subsidized essentially by the environment through factors such as cheap energy costs which do not internalize the true environmental costs of resource loss and pollution. If energy (and therefore capital) costs accurately reflected their true costs, then a switch back to labour usage would occur, increasing employment and reducing environmental damage.

The word production is, of course, quite misleading. When we talk of production we take it to mean the creation of something new. In actual fact, production is really about changes in the state of things: one substance or form is converted into another. Thus production is really about conversion, and any creation which takes place must be associated with destruction. Now, if we begin to see production as inevitably destructive, it takes on a much more negative connotation. This is not to advocate that all production should be ceased, only that production is only truly justified when the value of the product outweighs the value of that which is destroyed. This can be linked to the concept of product justifiability (Welford, 1996) where companies might be expected to consult with a wide range of stakeholders about the needs and costs of a product. This is likely to be linked to full life-cycle assessments of products.

Sustainable production needs to be matched with sustainable consumption if the outcome is to be truly effective. More sustainable consumption, of course, requires individuals as well as businesses to accept a good degree of responsibility themselves. Not everything can be left to businesses, and more and more people have to recognize that more consumption does not make you happy. Moreover, higher levels of consumption in the North simply contribute to the unhappiness of people in the South, who are impacted by the globalization trend. There is, nevertheless, a huge role which businesses can play through education. Perhaps more than any other institution in the world, business has a direct communications line with millions of people: its consumers. Linking marketing with education and campaigning is capable of influencing people in a more direct way than any educator or individual campaigner could ever hope for. Think about the impact that a corporation like Coca-Cola could have if it printed an environmental message on every can and bottle of Coke which it sold. We return to the important issue of education below.

As a start, however, sustainable production and consumption requires there to be a wider involvement of all company stakeholders in a move towards sustainable development. A transparent, pluralist approach facilitates this and allows for a degree of accountability through an assessment of progress, using techniques such as social auditing. Thus, social auditing takes account of not only the internal pluralism within an organization, but external pluralism as well. It also supports a greater degree of organizational transparency as advocated by Welford (1996). Social auditing is therefore a process to induce and promote new forms of democracy and accountability in the workplace and beyond.

The rationale behind using a social auditing approach for a business wishing to move towards sustainability is to acknowledge the rights of information to a wide constituency – that is, to attend to societal pluralism. Firms using the social audit process would be conceived of as lying at the centre of a network of social relationships which are articulated in a manner which is akin to a stakeholder model. Stakeholders are commonly understood to be those groups or individuals who can affect or are affected by the organization's social performance and objectives (Freeman, 1984). Put another way, social auditing recognizes the concepts of stewardship and accountability, and this in turn acknowledges that the whole of society has rights to information about actions taken on its behalf – for example, by businesses. Thus the social auditing process allows the business to engage with its stakeholders (representing, in part, societal interests), listen to and respond to their views and, where necessary, explain and justify its actions. But it is not only a one-way flow. Businesses are also able to influence their stakeholders so that the ultimate outcome is derived from consensus.

Respect for pluralism is developed as organizations become more transparent. That is, information is used to reduce the distance between the organization and the external (and internal) participants so that stakeholders can 'see into' the organization, assess what it is doing with the resources that determine future options and react (or not react) accordingly. As Gray (1994) argues, the impact of this information on this constituency, and their associated response, can be assumed to encourage the new practices which are necessary for sustainable development. If accountability and transparency are embraced, the corporation will find itself more closely in tune with its wider constituents and the company will develop its culture from a recognition of different stakeholder expectations and needs. But this is by no means an easy process. There will be trade-offs that have to be made if sustainability is to be pursued.

The social audit process means that employees' (internal stakeholders') values and expectations are accounted for alongside other external stakeholders' values and expectations. The social audit provides a medium in which the employees' values and expectations can be measured against other employees from different departments, levels or backgrounds, as well as against various other stakeholders. The resulting deeper appreciation of the diverse stakeholder pressures upon a company breeds a greater respect and trust between stakeholders. A relationship characterized by trust and mutual respect is a fruitful basis for employee participation. An open dialogue between management and employees on raised problems is necessary to deal with conflicts and resistance.

The social audit gives an employee a chance to compare and contrast core company values not only with their own values but with other employees' and other external stakeholders' values and expectations. The importance to a social audit of an overarching and explicit values framework written in terms of corporate values, visions, aims and objectives must be stressed. This is important because it provides the basic parameters for the ongoing dialogue between the various stakeholders and management. An explicit values framework avoids the anarchic flaws of this type of 'accounting receptivity'. In other words, it avoids a business degenerating into an unmanageable scramble of values, multiple aims and multiple measures of performance. In this way a firm can provide a sustainable direction to its activities.

Sustainable development at the corporate level

There exists a strange and fruitless search for a single definition of sustainable development among people who do not fully understand that we are really talking here of a process rather than a tangible outcome. This search is most apparent among positivist researchers who grope for a hard core of definitions and data which they can manipulate to produce simple solutions and singular answers to very complex concepts. Such simplifications cannot exist in the postmodern world and they simply hide a scientific research bias which is not appropriate to a highly political issue such as sustainable development. The search for a single definition of this concept is futile even though it may maintain the employment of a few academics.

Many argue that the concept of sustainable development is not appropriate to analysis at the corporate level. It is commonly argued that it can only be analysed and measured within a spatial dimension. While that may be true, it is nevertheless important to recognize that the business is central to the sustainable development process and that, therefore, we ought to be able to conceive of a framework whereby the firm would be operating at least in a way which is consistent with moves to sustainable development. That is what we do here.

Therefore, strategies are needed to translate conceptual ideas into practical reality. This requires a more radical assessment of environ-

69

mental strategy than we have seen to date. The challenge that faces the economic system is how to continue to fulfil its vital role within modern society while ensuring sustainability. The emphasis to date has been on piecemeal moves towards environmental improvement and this move has often been in the wrong direction. Here I advocate a model which is a combination of many different people's work and has developed over the last couple of years. It is based on six Es, consisting of the environment, empowerment, economics, ethics, equity and education. We can view these as six areas where the business should have a clear policy and agenda for change. This model is essentially a 'policy in, reporting out' framework where the activities of the firm are transparent. In other words, the business is expected to have a policy in each of these six areas to operationalize that policy using traditional corporate environmental management tools and a social auditing methodology (see below), and then to report on progress. Like all the models presented here, no firm will be able to produce a perfect profile in all six areas (even if that could be defined). Reports should detail progress in each element and demonstrate a degree of continuous improvement. They should also point to areas which still require attention, and produce objectives and targets for the next reporting period. It is worth briefly reviewing the sorts of idealized outcomes which the business should move towards in each of these six areas.

Environment

The environment is to be protected with the minimum use of non-renewable resources. Environmental performance will be monitored and measured, and it is likely that there will be an environmental management system in place with regular audit activity. Products will be assessed according to a life-cycle assessment and redesigned where practicable to reduce environmental impact. Products will also undergo a functionality assessment to determine whether there is a better way of providing the benefits of the product. There will be strong connections along the supply chain to integrate all stages of the product's life. After production, firms will manage, as far as possible, the use and disposal of the product through product stewardship procedures. Much emphasis will be placed on local action, including close connections with local community initiatives and protection of the health and safety of all employees and neighbours.

Empowerment

Everybody must feel part of the process of improvement, and must be empowered to recognize and act on their own obligations as well as work together closely with colleagues. There will be a strong participation in the workforce with respect to decision-making, profit-sharing and ownership structures. The organization will be open to new suggestions made by anyone in the workforce and workers will be rewarded on the basis of contribution to this overall ethos as well as work done. Human capital will be valued and workers will not be treated as simple factors of production. There will be enshrined rights within the organization relating to equal opportunities and individual freedoms. Diversity will be encouraged, not stifled.

Economy

The economic performance of the firm will be sustainable in that it will be sufficient to provide for on-going survival, the continued provision of employment, the payment of dividends to shareholders and the payment of fair wages to all concerned in the organization. Financial audits will be extended to a justification of profits made and a demonstration that they have been made through good business practices rather than through cost-cutting exploitation. There will be periodic new investment in physical capital as well as human capital (through education and retraining). Business relationships should be mutually advantageous to all parties concerned so that supply chain stability exists. Jobs are a central part of sustainability, and the provision and growth of employment is to be encouraged. Products made will be of good quality, durable and suitable for the purpose for which they were intended.

Ethics

The organization will have a clear set of values which it will publish and which will be periodically reassessed through the social audit process. The firm will be honest at all times and will be open to questions about its ethical stance, providing evidence relating to any activities which are being challenged. It will be a transparent organization and relations with subsidiaries, contractors and agents clearly identified. Ethics are not just something which the organization declares; it must translate them into practice via codes of conduct, education, communication and information. Businesses serve a variety of purposes for different stakeholders. Therefore we might argue that as a necessary condition, business activities are justifiable only in so far as they can be shown to meet the legitimate requirements of stakeholders.

Equity

Issues associated with equity exist both within and outwith the organization. Closely linked with empowerment issues there must be a clear statement of rights and equal opportunities within the firm. Trade along the supply chain must be equitable and, particularly with regard to international trade, there must be assurances for workers in developing countries, for indigenous populations and for human rights. End price audits of goods, whereby a product's final price is broken down into an analysis of who gets what share of that price, have been immensely valuable and can be used to demonstrate that subsistence wages being paid to the poor in developing countries is not the whole basis of the product's provision. The distribution of the benefits of product (or service) provision must be demonstrated as being just. Where appropriate, the firm will be involved in wider development initiatives through technology and know-how transfer, sponsorship, charitable donations and the provision of development aid to partners in developing countries.

Education

Education is at the root of the sustainable development process. We will make little progress without being able to communicate the challenge and to educate people to live in a more sustainable manner. Every business has to accept that it can be an educator because of its close links with both employees and customers, and should be providing suitable information and education to anyone working for it or purchasing its products and services. The firm can also be involved in community initiatives and wider public campaigns, and be part of the process to raise awareness more generally. It can work closely with campaign groups and non-governmental organizations through general cooperation, more specific sponsorship, the secondment of staff and similar initiatives. It is capable of bringing about much more sustainable consumption.

The six-Es approach, therefore, provides a set of ideals which the company can work towards. It contains a number of values and issues which are too commonly ignored in business; in many respects it challenges the business to accept a much wider responsibility for all its actions. The starting point is simply for management to think about these issues and, through interaction with the workforce, to produce policy statements in each of the six areas. However, that must be followed by concerted action as the business seeks out the road towards sustainability.

Competitive advantage through social and environmental differentiation

The nature of globalization and the fact that companies in developing countries have grown rapidly through gaining international competitiveness cannot be ignored. Thus, any form of corporate environmental management adopted in companies in the developing countries must be fully consistent with or even enhance competitive advantage. Here there needs to be a shift in the social and environmental emphasis. Rather than see corporate environmental management within the 'business-as-usual' context (which is what ecomodernism does), the environment and the concept of sustainable development can actually be at the forefront of competitiveness strategies, driving environmental, social and economic performance in positive directions. Rather than put the emphasis of competitiveness on cost reduction strategies, which we have seen already are often inconsistent with sustainable development, there is a need to see competitiveness enhanced through a degree of differentiation which is, in fact, fully consistent with sustainable development.

Many companies in developing countries have been very successful at increasing their competitiveness, making them, in many cases, world leaders in the industries in which they operate. The maintenance of that competitiveness is vital for the continued success of such firms. It is sometimes assumed that strategies and tools associated with environmental protection and sustainable development will be costly and may reduce such competitiveness. But here it is argued that operationalizing the types of changes advocated in the previous two sections can actually add to, rather than detract from, competitive advantage.

The trend towards globalization and the removal of barriers provides a new framework for competition. This is imposing a need for strategic reorientation by companies. It is my contention that environmental management and sustainable development at the corporate level, along with their associated strategies and tools, provide one effective method to increase the competitiveness of companies which see care of the environment as a new and integral part of business operations. Moreover, as technology matures and quality issues become a standard for doing business, environmental management and social responsibility provide a new impetus for the firm to gain advantage over its competitors. While some of those strategies might reduce costs (the ubiquitous win-win situation), that is not the emphasis here. Rather, more attention is placed on the area of differentiation where social and environmental aspects of sustainable development will have most impact as consumers become more and more sophisticated and as responsibility is increasingly expected of businesses.

Differentiation relates to the ways in which a company and its products are perceived. Differentiation consistent with sustainable development therefore requires a company to:

1 develop sound environmental and social performance;
2 engage in effective and educational marketing and distribution strategies; and
3 communicate its performance in a transparent and honest way to stakeholders.

Thus, if differentiation strategies can improve both the competitiveness of firms and their social and environmental performance, then we have a clear Pareto improvement. What is more, if firms are able to further differentiate their products and corporate image through sustainable production and accountability strategies, and by reporting on their performance in relation to sustainable development (via the six Es or some other model), then we can see how, working within modern global economies, sustainable development and environmental protection might actually be facilitated by companies. This goes much further than the corporate environmental management strategies which are associated with the more popular ecomodernist approaches. While competitive strategies to enhance sustainable development may seem inevitable, given increased consumer sophistication, pressure from competitors and along supply chains, there are nevertheless ways in which the process can be accelerated. This inevitably means considering the arena of environmental policy. We therefore now return to macro-level considerations and examine the sorts of policy changes which can both reduce the conflict between the international economic order and, at the same time, encourage businesses to think and act in a way which is more consistent with sustainable development.

POLICY FRAMEWORKS CAPABLE OF ENHANCING COMPETITIVE ADVANTAGE

Companies are dynamic and capable of responding to change in productive and innovative ways. Indeed Porter and van der Linde (1995) effectively show that changes in environmental policy can bring about significant environmental improvements as firms adjust their activities and innovate to avoid the costs and penalties of regulation and market measures. There is a need to develop a policy framework which is capable of stimulating the sorts of changes advocated in the previous three sections of this chapter. In particular, we would want to find ways of pushing businesses towards activities which are more consistent with sustainable production and consumption, rewarding moves towards sustainable development, and encouraging competitive strategies which can deliver such change. While there is insufficient room here for a full analysis of all possible policy changes, we would highlight three areas for consideration: environmental taxes, social accounting procedures and consumer information, and targeted protectionism.

Environmental taxes

Few would disagree with the proposition that the environment is undervalued because in many instances it represents a free good. Moreover, because the capitalist system is unable to account fully for long timescales, many non-renewable resources are also massively undervalued and used in a completely unsustainable way. These relatively simple arguments make taxes on environmental damage very attractive.

However, there are even more compelling arguments for the introduction of environmental taxes when one recognizes that the consequence of the environment actually subsidizing production activities (through raw materials and particularly energy) is to make labour increasingly expensive and uncompetitive in relation to capital. This situation is compounded when one considers that virtually all governments receive very large amounts of their taxation revenue from income taxes on workers and taxes levied on employers for employing labour.

Thus, a shift away from taxes on employment (which must be seen as a good) and towards taxes on environmental damage (a bad) must be regarded as a Pareto improvement. Moreover, taxes on inputs into production processes which are environmentally damaging would make them much more expensive relative to alternatives such as reuse, recycling, and so on.

Such fiscal readjustments will inevitably lead to more sustainable production activities. But they will also stimulate firms to find more environmentally responsible ways of producing goods if they are to maintain their competitiveness. The total tax take from the company need not increase (and may decrease) since increases in materials and energy costs will be associated with decreases in labour costs (direct employment taxes will fall and wages will also fall as decreased income taxes make it increasingly likely that workers will be prepared to take jobs at lower gross wages).

Social accounting procedures and consumer information

At the moment few companies are engaging in social accounting or social auditing. Those that have done so reported considerable benefits, however. If more standardized procedures existed for social accounting and reporting, a benchmark would be created for all firms to follow. Moreover, this would provide for standardized information which could be provided for consumers. An extension of the International Standards Organization's work on environmental performance evaluation (ISO 14031) would be a good starting point.

With the cooperation of industry, such reporting could become a standard. Procedures for verification would ensure useful consumer information with which to make more informed choices. Once again, however, it is capable of increasing the competitiveness of companies which are able to publish the most impressive reports and are thus able (in an objective way) to differentiate their corporate image from that of others. Social and environmental accountability and policies in line with sustainable development then become an integral part of the profile of a firm. Moreover, those companies which are unable to provide adequate information are more likely to be targeted by consumer groups, which can organize effective boycott activities.

Targeted protectionism

While the globalized economy may be with us and firmly embedded in the economic development of developing countries, it is nevertheless the case that some companies may be able to provide goods at cheap prices by ignoring social and environmental responsibilities. Thus, free trade will tend to encourage the activities of unscrupulous companies (or their associate companies whose activities are easier to hide) who can drive down costs through human and ecological exploitation. In such circumstances, targeted protectionism is not only justified, it is to be encouraged. It is widely accepted that the activities of many large transnational corporations are too difficult to control and that the nomadic nature of much of their capital means that they often have more power than the governments which are supposed to regulate them. However, while it may be difficult to control their production activities, it is relatively easy to control their markets. And without their markets they cannot exist. Thus, consumer activities and boycotts as suggested above need greater support, and appropriate action at a national or international level can be taken against companies until they put right misconduct. Companies whose markets are potentially threatened will soon adopt policies which prevent this from happening.

CONCLUSIONS

This chapter has suggested that many large companies (including some in developing countries) are adopting corporate environmental management strategies and tools. While this is to be encouraged, the chapter expresses some doubt about the real effectiveness of many of the tools being used. Although companies may perceive themselves to be doing things right, therefore, we must nevertheless ask whether they are doing the right thing. It was pointed out that the trend of ecomodernism may not be sufficient if our aim is to bring about a situation which is consistent with sustainable development.

Nevertheless, we have demonstrated that the fault cannot be attributed entirely to business alone. Businesses often struggle with a globalized economic order which is inconsistent with sustainable development and which forces them continually to drive down costs in order to survive. In such a system it is little wonder that businesses view environmental protection and social responsibility as a relatively low priority. Nevertheless, in a world where businesses are increasingly powerful and in a world where they are actually able to create more effective change than many governments, we should still expect them to take a lead.

Thus we are left with the question relating to what companies ought to try to achieve. We must recognize that we live in an increasingly globalized economy where companies will only survive if they can maintain a degree of competitive advantage. But rather than see this as a barrier to social and environmental improvement and a step towards sustainable development, we ought to regard it as an opportunity. In this respect, companies can build upon the competitive advantage which already exists, stressing real differentiation strategies associated with environmental protection and social responsibility. Through a greater degree of accountability and transparency, and effective communications, they can create a new norm which requires every business to perform in a way which is more consistent with sustainable development.

This chapter therefore advocates a clear definition of sustainable development as applied to the corporate setting and sets out a model which is consistent with this aim. It calls on companies to pursue policies of sustainable production, producing less of higher quality, reducing environmental and social impacts, and increasing levels of employment. Social accounting and social auditing are seen as a way of tracking and reporting on achievements in this area and this in turn will help to differentiate the corporate image of the company, leading to a degree of competitive advantage. This is going to be very challenging for businesses, but there are signs that businesses are responding to this challenge. With the growth of information available about firms (provided both by themselves and their detractors) on media such as the Internet, it will be much easier for consumers to make informed choices about the products they buy. Moreover, as crises associated with environmental degradation and social conflict increase, so too will the demands from individuals for change. Changes in civil society, with NGOs and coalitions of individuals being more willing to assert their power, will put a whole range of new pressures on business.

Policies which are consistent with such aspirations are nevertheless still required to accelerate the move towards a situation which is more consistent with sustainable development. These policies include the need for the widespread introduction of environmental taxes, the development of a framework for social auditing and consumer information, and targeted protectionism against companies which can be identified as consistently underperforming or unnecessarily exploiting humans or the ecological base.

The proposals advocated in this chapter go far beyond the aspirations and tools associated with ecomodernism and ecoefficiency. Nevertheless they work within the existing globalized economy where companies in developing countries will be able to develop effective and efficient strategies which enhance their competitive positioning. We must challenge the ecomodernists to do more, to throw away their own highly restrictive assumptions and models, and to take the next big leap forward in engaging with sustainable development. This is both achievable and necessary.

At present, however, this chapter argues that we see a very 'disturbing development'. Interestingly, the word 'disturbing' has two different meanings and both are appropriate to the situation as described here. Firstly, the dominant trends of corporate environmentalism, globalization and free trade are disturbing in that they are worrying. They conflict with the process of sustainable development and act as a serious impediment to any change which is consistent with that concept. Secondly, the conflicts inherent between sustainable development, the international economic order and corporate environmentalism are disturbing in as much as they may be disrupting what otherwise might be progressive development in the South. This is because the emphasis on cost reduction in the globalized marketplace requires a degree of underdevelopment in low wage economies in order to satisfy the needs of the North and wealthy élites in the South. Unless we can tackle the conflicts at the root of the international economic order, therefore, 'disturbing development' will continue.

Chapter 4

Towards Sustainable Production and Consumption: from Products to Services

(written with C William Young)

INTRODUCTION

There has been much debate about the appropriate tools for the improvement of the environmental performance of companies. We have seen the introduction of environmental management systems and their associated standards, environmental auditing and reporting, and tools focusing on the environmental performance of products such as life-cycle assessment. These tools have been most often applied to manufacturing industries and tangible products. However, there is now a need to go further than simply addressing the environmental performance of companies if our aim is to be sustainable development. This chapter therefore seeks to address the issues of corporate responsibility in the context of sustainable development. It questions the appropriateness and efficacy of contemporary corporate environmental management tools alone and investigates the ways in which all businesses can respond better to the demands of the sustainable development agenda. The emphasis of the analysis also moves us away from the traditional manufacturing sector towards the examining services.

Examining service provision is an underdeveloped and under-researched area of the corporate environmental management and sustainable development debate. However, we also select the service sector for particular attention because there is increased interest among firms in putting less emphasis on the supply of a particular product and more interest in the provision of a service, of which that product may be a part. In so doing there is often an assumption that service provision is likely to be less environmentally damaging. While this may be the case, we see little reason why it should necessarily be better for progress towards sustainable development, however.

Businesses do find the concept of sustainable development hard to operationalize. After a European survey of how the world's more environmentally advanced companies are reacting to the emerging issue of sustainable development, Bebbington and Gray (1996) provide some conclusions:

1 Most companies have yet to examine fully the nature of sustainable development and its implications for current business practice. The vast majority of companies are treating sustainable development as an (implicit) extension of environmental management.
2 While companies do not appear to have embraced fully all the ecoefficiency implications of sustainable development, they do seem sensitive to and in support of the ecojustice elements of the concept.
3 A much clearer set of guidance given to businesses worldwide on what sustainable development may mean for business.
4 Conflicts from the constraints of actions towards sustainable development are more likely to occur in accounting/performance-centred and large organizations than value-centred and smaller or decentralized companies.
5 The use of life-cycle assessment and/or the ecobalance approaches to analysing the company's interaction with society and the environment seems to offer considerable, valuable promise.
6 The central message about the assistance that accounting systems and measurement frameworks can provide to companies addressing environmental issues has not yet been received fully.

Eden (1994) suggests that public trust in environmental information provided by business is weak. This does not mean directly that the demand for environmentally marketed products and services will decline, but it does mean that businesses must do more to provide the information which consumers and other stakeholders need to make more informed judgements. This is even more the case if one considers moves towards the provision of goods and services which have characteristics which are consistent with sustainable development. More significantly, public distrust may contribute to social and political pressure for widening and strengthening social and environmental regulations and voluntary standards as a means to ground the legitimacy of business actions.

In this chapter, therefore, we contribute to the debate over useful frameworks and measurement systems which can be used to provide meaningful information to stakeholders. We do this by extensive reference to literature on environmental and sustainable development frameworks, recognized approaches to the measurement and indicators of sustainable development, and some literature on social auditing. From this we derive a workable framework which can both track progress towards operations which are consistent with sustainable development and engage in stakeholder dialogue.

While it may not be entirely appropriate to define what sustainable development means at the level of the firm, we take the view nevertheless that it is important to give firms and their stakeholders some indication of how they can play their part in bringing about a society based on the principles of sustainable development. Therefore, our assertion is that it is possible to define a set of principles by which the firm can assess and track progress. This requires us to examine the activities of the firm which would be consistent with a move towards sustainable development in a wider sense and to put in place some sort of measurement and reporting framework. We do this in the context of the service sector where emphasis is placed on sustainable production and consumption within a supply chain framework. Thus, after some consideration of the service sector in general, the chapter considers definitions of sustainable development at the firm level, measurement, reporting and dialogue instruments and then presents an extension of the framework developed in the previous chapter which can be used by companies in both monitoring their own performance and reporting this to stakeholders.

CHARACTERISTICS OF THE SERVICE SECTOR

A good starting point is therefore to consider the characteristics of the service sector and to consider how it differs from the manufacturing sector. Here we consider three issues. Firstly, we must consider the basic intangibility of services (as opposed to the concreteness of manufacturing goods): services cannot be stocked; they cannot be demonstrated easily; and while they can be sold, there is not necessarily any transfer of ownership. Secondly, most services actually consist of acts and interactions. Thirdly, the production and consumption of a service cannot always be kept apart clearly, since they generally occur simultaneously and at the same place. Further differences in the characteristics of the two sectors can be seen in Table 4.1 (Normann, 1984).

Even with service companies with material services (like hotels and catering, repair work or cleaning) which require material resources and energy, the overall material metabolism effect of the service sector is generally quite small compared to all non-service industries because interaction processes between supplier and user, be they material or

Table 4.1 *Some Typical Differences between Manufacturing Industry and Service Industry*

Manufacturing	Service
1 The product is generally concrete	1 The service is immaterial
2 Ownership is transferred when a purchase is made	2 Ownership is not generally transferred
3 The product can be resold	3 The product cannot be resold
4 The product can be demonstrated before purchase	4 The product cannot usually be effectively demonstrated (it does not exist before purchase)
5 The product can be stored by sellers and buyers	5 The product cannot be stored
6 Consumption is preceded by production	6 Production and consumption generally coincide
7 Production, selling and consumption are locally differentiated	7 Production, consumption and often even selling are spatially united
8 The product can be transported	8 The product cannot be transported (though 'producers' often can)
9 The seller produces	9 The buyer/client takes part directly in the production
10 Indirect contact is possible between company and client	10 In most cases direct contact is necessary
11 Can be exported	11 The service cannot be exported normally, but the service delivery system can

Source: Normann, 1984, p8

informational services, basically require little more than premises, buildings, heating and lighting (Ellger and Scheiner, 1997). Nevertheless, there are other social and ethical impacts of service provision and these should not be ignored if our aim is to move towards activities which are consistent with sustainable development.

In many ways, it may be easier actually to deal with the impacts in the service sector because of the close proximity of the buyer and seller and the fact that the ownership of the service is not generally transferred (meaning that the originator has more control over the use of a service rather than the use of a product, and because production and consumption generally coincide). These characteristics imply that a supply chain approach to analysing the impacts of services upon some measure of sustainable development may be very effective.

Two further questions deserve special attention when one attempts to assess the environmental impact of the 'service society', however. Firstly, we must consider the servicing versus self-servicing relationship. With comparatively high costs for labour and much lower costs for material consumption and capital, services are often replaced by purchases of material goods and associated 'self-servicing' by consumers (automatic teller machines, Internet travel agencies, etc). Similarly, in modern self-service retailing, the special packaging of individual objects, a theft-preventive measure, makes retailing less labour and more material intensive than it would be. In a situation where energy, material resources and capital are comparatively cheap, labour becomes extremely expensive, and there may be quite severe employment issues to be addressed in the shift towards a more service-oriented economy. In other words, there is a degree to which more capital will be employed to deliver services at the expense of jobs. One solution might be to see changes in taxation (shifting taxation from labour to energy, for example) which would certainly shift production from manufacturing to services in a way that generated jobs rather than lost them (Ellger and Scheiner, 1997). Although that debate is beyond the scope of this chapter, nevertheless we consider the employment aspects of sustainable production and consumption as crucial.

Secondly, an intrinsic environmental problem of services seems to be the transport problem: services are, necessarily, interactions between the supply and demand sides. In many cases, apart from telecommunicative interaction, services often demand the co-presence of supplier and user, their physical get together, so that 'change' of the user or his/her object can be brought about. Thus, increasing service processes means increasing interaction and often results in increasing transport: goods transport (in material services, including trade of goods) and passenger transport (personal services, élite communication services) (Ellger and Scheiner, 1997). Hence, we stress once again the need for a supply chain approach which would be capable of internalizing such supply *and* demand considerations into our framework of analysis.

Notwithstanding these issues, some assumptions do seem to have been made relating to the impacts of the service sector. Lundgren (1996) agrees that the predominant view of companies in the service sector is that the environment is either not affected at all or that it is affected only to a minor degree. The direct effects are regarded to be very small and the indirect effects, most often, are not seen at all. Figure 4.1 illustrates the degree of materialization and direct effects caused by the manufacturing sector and the service sector. The service sector contains 'white collar' businesses as a subset of the whole, which relate to companies run from the office desk, such as insurance and banking.

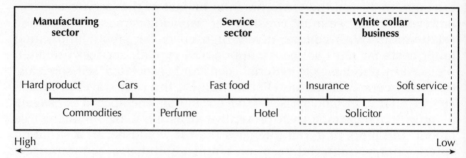

Note: The product–service continuum with the white collar business as part of the service sector and its degree of materialization and amount of direct effects caused (adapted from Irons, 1994, p10 and Lundgren, 1996, p5).

Figure 4.1 *The Product–Service Continuum*

Other surveys seem to confirm the view that service sector companies do not perceive there to be significant environmental issues which need to be addressed. The main conclusions from the Norwegian GRIP-Barometer (Ytterhus and Refsum, 1996) which conducted a Norwegian survey were that the service sector has not implemented environmental programmes to the same extent as manufacturing firms.

However, in this chapter we do not consider environmental issues alone since that represents only part of the sustainable development agenda. Numerous commentators have discussed the need for social and ethical aspects of firm behaviour to be included in any analysis. Here the difference between service companies and manufacturing may be less easy to differentiate. A large financial services company may be dealing indeed with rather more social and ethical issues than a comparably sized engineering company. These 'other' aspects of sustainable development therefore need to be defined and considered as equally important in the service sector.

FRAMEWORKS FOR FIRM-LEVEL DEFINITIONS OF SUSTAINABLE DEVELOPMENT, PRODUCTION AND CONSUMPTION

Our aim in this chapter is to derive a conceptual framework which is capable of defining activities at the firm level and which would be consistent with a move towards sustainable development. We do that by considering both sustainable production (which we use as shorthand for production activities which are consistent with a move towards sustainable development) and sustainable consumption (similarly, a shorthand for consumption activities which are consistent with a move towards sustainable development). Although nothing may be actually produced in many parts of the service sector, we continue to use the term production because it is commonly understood to stand for the development, definition and provision of a service.

Our approach also puts great emphasis on the need to communicate with stakeholders in a two-way flow of information. Clearly different stakeholders will be involved in a complex process of precisely defining these terms. According to the World Business Council for Sustainable Development:

> *Sustainable production and consumption involves business, government, communities and households contributing to environmental quality through the efficient production and use of natural resources, the minimization of wastes, and the optimization of products and services.* (WBCSD, 1996, p10)

However, this is too narrow a definition since it falls into the (common) trap of equating sustainable development only with environmental quality. We would argue that sustainable development (because it is a 'development' concept) should focus on quality of life and that a better definition might be that sustainable production and consumption is:

> *... the use of goods and services that respond to basic needs and bring a better quality of life, while minimizing the use of natural resources, toxic materials and emissions of waste and pollutants over the life cycle, so as not to jeopardize the needs of future generations.* (Norwegian Ministry of the Environment, 1994)

Salim (1994) agrees with this approach because it emphasizes future generations as well as present ones and goes further in suggesting that: ·

> *Sustainable consumption implies that the consumption of current generations as well as future generations improves in quality. Such a concept of consumption requires the optimization of consumption subject to maintaining services and quality of resources and the environment over time.* (Salim, 1994)

As we outlined in the previous section, a useful approach to operationalizing sustainable production and consumption is nevertheless to consider it as a function of supply side activities and demand side activities:

> *The emphasis of sustainable production is on the supply side of the equation, focusing on the improving environmental performance in key economic sectors, such as agriculture, energy, industry, tourism, and transport. Sustainable consumption addresses the demand side, looking at how the goods and services required to meet basic needs and improve quality of life – such as food and health, shelter, clothing, leisure and mobility – can be delivered in ways that reduce the burden on the Earth's carrying capacity.* (Robins and Roberts, 1997)

Sustainable production is seen as production which is economically, environmentally and socially responsible. Moreover, 'economically responsible' might be defined as both economic for the producer (ie profitable) and for those involved in the production process (ie in relation to fair wages, employment, etc). Thus, another useful definition of sustainable production is as follows:

> *To produce less of higher quality and durability with much lower environmental and social impacts at higher levels of employment, while making an acceptable profit or surplus.* (Welford, 1997)

As a starting point, we review a number of attempts by people to derive frameworks which would be of use to business in the adoption of practices which are consistent with a move towards sustainable development. In undertaking such a review, we attempt to pull together common strands in order to define an overarching approach which would have a good degree of consensus. However, the frameworks themselves should provide the reader with some ideas for choosing appropriate indicators of performance in specific sectors. We have chosen to examine ten frameworks which seem to have had some prominence in the literature in this area. Because of the underdeveloped literature on the social aspects of sustainable development (as opposed to environmental ones), some of the frameworks deal only with environmental issues.

Framework 1 – The Norwegian Ministry of the Environment (1995)

The Norwegian Ministry of the Environment (1995) suggests that at the enterprise level companies need to strengthen their environmental efforts by actions such as:

1   Business as a consumer:
    • Set an example by integrating environmental criteria and targets into supplier and purchasing policies.
    • Build and spread experience in maximizing ecoefficiency in the consumption of energy and resources.
2   Business as producer, financier and retailer:
    • Rethink product and process innovation and technology development programmes to include sustainable consumption factors.
    • Explore the market potential of substituting traditional products with new environmental services in repair, reconditioning (including upgrading), recycling and remanufacturing.
    • Supply goods and services with a product declaration containing information on key environmental parameters (eg durability, repairability, energy and water use, toxic contents).
    • Extend producer responsibility through increased product lifespans and improved after-sales service provision, followed by upgrading, reuse or recycling.
    • Reduce energy consumption, material intensity and waste at the design stage.
    • Integrate the need to promote sustainable consumption into advertising, marketing and product information (eg through independent verification of advertising claims).
    • Incorporate the goals of more sustainable consumption and production in undertaking technology transfer to developing countries and countries with economies in transition.
    • Promote the development of practical applications to internalize environmental costs through full resource cost pricing and environmental accounting efforts.
    • Integrate the environmental costs of production process into the price of products, including the costs of environmental liability.

Here much emphasis is put on supply chain initiatives, including procurement procedures and sales service provision. It also raises issues associated with relationships with developing countries, which is an important part of the sustainable development agenda. In terms of services, it is suggested that enterprises in the financial sector, such as banks and insurance companies, should incorporate environ-mental risk and ecoefficiency criteria and goals into the assessment and management of their services for both individual and business consumers. Enterprises in the retail and distribution sectors should assist their customers through the provision of accurate information on the environmental impacts of goods and services and facilities for materials recovery, recycling and reuse. They should use their intermediate position to influence the supply of environmentally sound goods and services.

Framework 2 – Gladwin et al (1995)

Redirecting and reframing corporations for social sustainability according to Gladwin et al (1995) demands strong transformational leadership within both governments and corporations. Corporate leaders will need to:

1   inspire shared visions of their enterprises as socially and environ-mentally sustainable;
2   create organizational cultures (ie values and thinking patterns) that guide and support sustainable behaviour;
3   encourage quick and effective organizational learning about the demands and opportunities (eg for new products, new market segments and new geographical emphases) presented by sustainable development;
4   empower and reward members of the organization to initiate and take responsibility for sustainable behaviour;
5   develop the organizational expertise (eg planning, assessment and measurement systems) necessary for performing sustainably;
6   persuade all stakeholders of the organization (eg shareholders, customers, suppliers, employees, etc) to support sustainable corporate behaviour;
7   help to transform public policies such that they reward sustainable development (eg reallocation of the 'peace dividend', full-cost pricing, expanded aid programmes and fiscal incentives for addressing human priority concerns, etc) and help to transform market mechanisms such that they reward 'caring, responsible and sustainable' commercial success.

Here the emphasis is on organizational change, empowerment, ethics, learning and education, and it is accepted that there is a need for clear measurement systems and performance frameworks. But there is also an interesting emphasis put on not only reporting performance to stakeholders but also actively influencing them, making them more supportive of an organization's sustainable development behaviour.

This requires two-way communications and the development of real dialogue.

Framework 3 – van Someren (1995)

In this framework we see an emphasis placed on forward planning in terms of time horizons and of integrating issues such as disposal, recycling and reuse into a strategy for products. It is a product oriented framework, but even in the service sector its emphasis on long-term planning horizons is worth bearing in mind as well as its emphasis on supply chain management.

Table 4.2 *Characteristics of the Ideal Sustainable Development Corporation*

1 Long-term view including:
a Knowledge about impacts and their duration
b Strategy (time horizon longer than 5–20 years)
c Investments
d Use of production factors
e Product lifetime
f Resource lifetime
2 Minimization of emissions and environmental impacts to an acceptable level or even to zero if necessary.
3 Minimization of disposal and waste.
4 Minimization of inputs given output (dematerialize).
5a Minimization of primary inputs.
5b Maximization of secondary inputs (recycling, reuse).
5c Closed material cycles.
6 Minimization of risk.
7 Creation of environmentally orientated innovations (product, process, organization).

Source: van Someren, 1995, p25

Framework 4 – Starik et al (1996)

According to Starik et al (1996) research has shown that designing and skilfully acting on strategic plans are often keys to organizational effectiveness. 'Seat of the pants' management has often been found to be a characteristic of mediocre or failed businesses, so the sensible strategic management manager typically goes through a process or set of steps in first constructing and then carrying out strategic plans.

A three-step process is suggested by Starik et al (1996) to develop an environmental strategy process called MOSAIC, which involves the company achieving the following:

- Initial: mission, objectives, strategic orientation, action plan, implementation, controls.
- Analysis: stakeholder focus, issue focus, sustainability.
- Improved: mission, objectives, strategic orientation, action plan, implementation, controls.

This three-step procedure includes a first step of identifying natural environmental interactions with an organization's current and recent missions, objectives, strategic postures, action plans, implementation mechanisms and control features. The second step is to assess ecological impact trends and predictions with its several natural environments. The third and final step is to combine the first two stages and begin to plan and then implement any necessary changes to the plan, and then implement any necessary changes to the organization's current MOSAIC for the future sustainability of both the organization and its natural environment to form the new MOSAIC (Starik et al, 1996).

This three-step process, with the MOSAIC concept at its core, advises managers to identify their current strategic environmental situations, to investigate actual and potential changes in stakeholders and issues and, finally, to develop strategic environmental responses to the combination of their current MOSAIC situations and future environmental conditions (Starik et al, 1996). This approach puts much emphasis on the importance of the implementation and subsequent controls with an ongoing analysis of stakeholders' demands.

Framework 5 – Shrivastava and Hart (1995)

This framework places great emphasis on the firm having a clear mission or vision. It sees deep change towards sustainable development as requiring the firm to have sustainability as a corporate purpose. Such a strategy must go further than both 'band-aid approaches' where end-of-pipe technology and pollution prevention are emphasized. It also proposes a framework which goes beyond more usual approaches (termed 'more serious') which see environmental stewardship as a core value. The emphasis needs to be on development in the South, full cost accounting procedures, and stakeholder integration where sustainability is a key performance indicator. This is summarized in Table 4.3.

Framework 6 – Welford (1997)

A three-dimensional approach to achieving sustainability in the business organization is to examine impacts on *people* (a broadly

Table 4.3 *Designing the Sustainable Corporation*

	Band-Aid	More Serious	Deep Change
Mission	Waste and emission reduction as goals	Environmental stewardship as a core value	Sustainability as corporate purpose
Strategy	Clean-up or divest polluting businesses	Invest in 'green' businesses/ products	Reduce material consumption in the North; develop markets in South
Competency	Deploy state-of-the-art 'green' production methods	Consortia or alliances to develop green technology	Reorientation of firm around sustainable competencies
Structure/ Systems	Environment as a function	Rewards for environmental performance	Full cost accounting
Processes/ Culture	Pollution prevention	Product stewardship; design for environment	Stakeholder integration
Performance	Environmental audit	Public disclosure of environmental performance	Sustainability as key performance indicator

Source: Shrivastava and Hart, 1995, p163

social dimension), the *planet* (broadly environmental) and *product* (which would include goods, services and profits, all as useful outputs). As a starting point we might see the whole purpose of business as revolving around the three 'Ps'. The main objective of a business is to make a range of *products* and/or to provide services in a way which generates profits. But it does this in the general context of having to work with a range of *people* through employment, supply chain linkages and as customers. It uses the basic resources of the *planet* as the material foundation of these very activities. The aim is therefore to maximize the benefits within this sort of activity while minimizing the disadvantages.

As a starting point, Table 4.4 outlines the targets for consideration under these three broad dimensions and suggests some tools of analysis which might be used. In terms of product (which we are defining much more widely than just material output), targets include goods produced, services provided and profits (or surpluses) made as a result of these activities. Indeed, we can include in this definition anything useful from an economic perspective. Tools such as life-cycle assessment allow us to track the impacts of our products more widely and to say something about the sources of raw materials and the ways in which they themselves were produced. We can easily build in social and ethical considerations here which might include the rights of indigenous populations, fair wages and fair trade arrangements, for example. A functionality assessment takes an even broader view of the firm's product. In asking questions such as what is this product for and is there a better alternative to providing the services which this product offers, we are forced to justify the usefulness of our outputs and to consider other alternatives which can provide the same results but at a lower environmental, social or financial cost.

In terms of people, the first responsibility of the firm must be to its own employees (particularly with regard to their health, safety, employment rights and continuity of employment) and then to the whole range of other stakeholders which the company has. Internally clear employment policies and audits of employment practices are a good starting point. Externally there needs to be stakeholder assessment, social audits and dialogue between the company and all interested parties.

More traditional environmental management techniques can be used when considering our third dimension, the planet. Environmental auditing is central here along with strategies such as the education of employees, customers and others, and, where appropriate, campaigning in a broader sense to contribute to the change necessary to reverse the environmental degradation of the planet.

Table 4.4 *Operationalizing the Three-Ps Model of Sustainable Development*

Dimension	Targets	Tools
Product	• Goods • Services • Profits/surpluses	• Life cycle assessment • Functionality assessment • Financial indicators/accounts
People	• Employment and employment practices • Other stakeholders	• Employment policies and audits • Stakeholder assessment and social audits
Planet	• Environmental improvement • Species protection	• Corporate environmental management tools • Environmental auditing • Education and campaigning

Source: Welford, 1997

One of the benefits of this model is that we can link targets to tools and, in turn, tools to reports. There is nothing here that has not been tried and tested by a number of firms. What only a few firms have done, however, is to put all these aspects together into a reporting framework specifically designed to track sustainability.

Framework 7 – Rydberg (1995)

In taking a broad life cycle approach, it is argued in this framework that the company can consider more easily its social, environmental and other obligations. Thus life-cycle assessment (LCA) covers long term environmental needs. Life-cycle cost (LCC) describes and assesses the economy of the product in the life cycle perspective, covering the economy of the product (the production phase or, in terms of services, the provision stage) and customer (use-phase). Quality function development (QFD) assesses the requirements of the user, relating to what extent the product fulfils the functional (and other) needs, generally known as 'quality'. Thus the three methods outlined in Figure 4.2 are complementary in covering the requirements of the customer, the producer, and society and the environment (Rydberg, 1995).

It is our view that this framework can be used in the service sector where the service needs of the customer, society and the environment

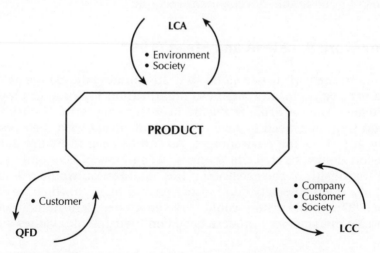

Key: LCA – life-cycle assessment, QFD – quality function deployment, LCC – life-cycle cost.
Source: Rydberg, 1995, p104

Figure 4.2 *An Indication of the Complementary Nature of the Tools in the Nordic Project in Addressing the Needs of the Company, the Customer, Society and the Environment*

are addressed. Like previous models it goes beyond simple production stages (or service provision stages) and requires the firm to think carefully about and assess the full life-cycle of the product or service, requiring effective supply chain management. It pulls together implicitly various stakeholders in some degree of two-way communications.

Framework 8 – Callens and Tyteca (1995)

Callens and Tyteca (1995) provide a framework which is made up essentially of performance indicators at various levels (see Table 4.5). Their approach is to consider four categories, the first three of which are economic, social and environmental indicators. These are perhaps the most commonly used in the literature on sustainable development. Welford (1997) also talks of the need for measures in the area of environmental, social and economic performance. Often these are integrated into an overall assessment of sustainable development. However, Callens and Tyteca (1995) argue that these only take into account particular aspects of sustainable development, which should incorporate all three kinds of considerations. A fourth, ultimate category, is also considered – namely, overall sustainable development indicators. Until now, these have been developed mainly at the global level, ie state or country level. There is clearly a need to consider what types of firm level behaviour are appropriate here in terms of sustainable development records.

Framework 9 – Stead and Stead (1992)

In this framework it is argued that sustainable development should be a core value in any business organization because it supports a strategic vision of firms surviving over the long term. It does this by integrating their need to earn an economic profit with their responsibility to protect the environment. As can be seen in Figure 4.3, such a vision demonstrates the interconnectedness of economic success and the health of the ecosystem; the organization would see itself as part of a greater society and natural environment to which its survival is tied. Thus, this vision would serve as an excellent foundation for a strategic management process based on instrumental values such as:

- wholeness – achieving a sustainable balance in our ecosystem is possible if the planet is viewed as an interconnected whole, a living system that can survive only if balance is maintained among its various subsystems;
- posterity – valuing posterity, believing that future generations of human beings are prominent factors in strategic decisions, can be

Table 4.5 *Examples of Existing Economic, Social, Environmental and Sustainability Indicators*

	Economic indicator	Social indicator	Environmental indicator	Sustainability indicator
Level 1: product, process	•Value added •Market share •Economic life cycle	•Labour intensity •Work conditions •Customer satisfaction	•LCA	
Level 2: plant, firm	•Value added •Profitability •Market share •Brand image •Turnover •Net production •Shipment value	•Work conditions •Labour intensity •Productivity •Employment •Average salaries •Salarial disparities •Work accidents •Absenteeism	•Environmental Impact Assessment •Productive efficiency •Performance indicators •Scientific indicators •Environmental accounting	•Sustainable development records
Level 3: state, country	•National output	•Net economic welfare •Unemployment	•Net national product •National environmental accounts	•Index of sustainable welfare •Indicator of weak sustainability

Source: Callens and Tyteca, 1995, p5

instrumental in attaining a sustainable economic and ecological balance;

• community – a community lies primarily in the complex cognitive networks that form around the values and expectations of the individuals and organizations that comprise it;

• quality – quality is not an absolute percentage of defective products, and so forth; rather it is an overall perception of what the firm's products and services should be. As such, quality serves as a guiding force behind the firm's operations and its relationship with its stakeholders; and

• smallness – humans live on a small planet, one that is becoming overburdened with population increases and economic activity; thus, thinking in terms of a smaller scale seems necessary.

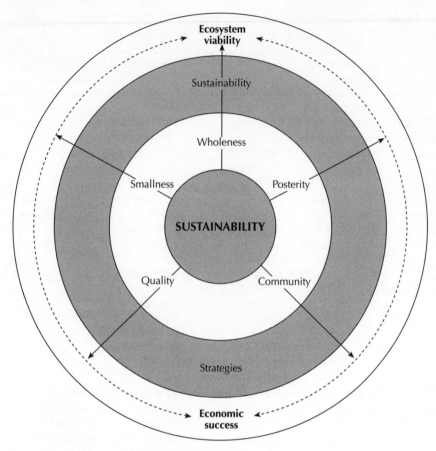

Source: Stead and Stead, 1992, p169

Figure 4.3 *Envisioning Sustainability Strategies*

A firm with a vision based on sustainability would develop strategies which were designed to enhance its long-run profitability as well as to protect the environment, called sustainability strategies (Stead and Stead, 1992).

Framework 10 – Returning to the six Es

In the previous chapter, a model was advocated which is a combination of many different people's work and brings together many of the issues discussed in the previous frameworks. Nevertheless it has the advantage of placing rather more emphasis on social and ethical issues than many of the earlier approaches did. This is consistent with the increasing acceptance of the need to address the social dimensions of sustainable development as much as the environmental ones. Table 4.6 summarizes the policy areas discussed and suggests tools for operationalizing a change process. The firm will not only use these tools to achieve its sustainable development objectives in these six areas but will also report on progress. This model is essentially a 'policy in, reporting out' framework, where the activities of the firm are transparent. In other words, the business is expected to have a policy in each of these six areas, to operationalize that policy using the indicative tools suggested in Table 4.6 and then to report on progress. Like all the models presented here, no firm will be able to produce a perfect profile in all six areas (even if that could be defined). Reports should detail progress in each element and demonstrate a degree of continuous improvement. They should also point to areas which still require attention and produce objectives and targets for the next reporting period.

Table 4.6 *Policy Areas and Tools for Sustainable Development*

Policy area	Indicative tools
Environment	Life cycle assessment Environmental management system and audits Functionality assessment Resource management
Empowerment	Teambuilding Participation Equal opportunities Declaration of rights
Economics	Profits/surplus Employment Quality Long term financial stability and investment
Ethics	Transparency of objectives Openness to concerns Honesty Values statement
Equity	Fair trade policy and activity End price auditing Development aid Sponsorship
Education	Training Customer information Community involvement Campaigning

MEASUREMENT FRAMEWORKS

All the frameworks discussed above need to be operationalized. It would be insufficient to present them to businesses without some idea of how they might be used. The frameworks do lend themselves to the use of indicators in order that progress towards sustainable development might be operationalized. In other words, the list of areas where the firm should be active needs to be matched by a framework of measurement and reporting such that progress towards policies which are consistent with sustainable development can be seen in an open and transparent way, capable of being assessed by various stakeholders.

James and Bennett (1994) discuss the measures of environment-related performance: why measure, what to measure, current approaches and how to measure. In the latter, a model in the form of a continuous loop consisting of eight stages of the development of environment-related performance measures is suggested (see Figure 4.4). This general approach can be extended to our framework of sustainable production and consumption.

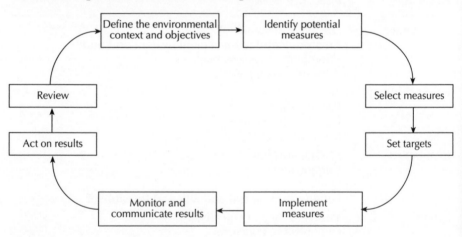

Source: James and Bennett, 1994, pp92–93

Figure 4.4 *A Continuous Loop of the Stages of Environment-related Performance Measurement*

The first stage, which defines the environmental context and objectives, states the organization's impact on the environment. Potential measures, including priority areas, are then identified in the second stage. Step three selects the measures by their appropriateness to their purpose, cost effectiveness, comparability and compatibility with other measures. In step four, the current position is established, targets are set and the feasibility of achieving this is assessed. The fifth stage implements the measures through systems that collect and report the information. It is important that the targets are communicated to the relevant staff and stakeholders, and that staff are empowered and resourced to achieve the targets. The results are monitored and communicated in the sixth step. The results may have to be verified internally and externally if they are to have any credibility with stakeholders. The seventh stage acts on the results, including identifying what changes are needed to improve the measures and results. The final and eighth stage reviews the overall performance measurement system, establishing if it works satisfactorily and if there are new areas where measurement is necessary. The process continues through stage one and back to the review, advancing the measures of environmental performance. In effect, this is an application of the usual continual improvement loop.

A state of the art environmental performance measurement framework consistent with the above approach, as well as being suitable for our purposes here (if it is extended to include all sustainable development issues), is the current version of the ISO 14031 guidelines scheduled to be released in 1999. The definition currently being adopted by the ISO for environmental performance evaluation (EPE) is a:

> *... process to facilitate management decisions regarding an organization's environmental performance by selecting indicators, collecting and analysing data, assessing information against environmental performance criteria, reporting and communicating, and periodic review and improvement of this process.* (ISO, 1997, p5)

The scope of the EPE guidelines is guidance on the design and the use of EPE. It describes the process of EPE, giving some examples of environmental performance indicators, though for illustrative purposes only. The guidelines do not establish environmental performance levels and are not intended for use as specification guidelines for certification/registration purposes. Equally, it is not our intention to define precise sustainable development indicators since these are most appropriately done at the industry level. However, this general approach can be applied to some sort of sustainable development framework.

The ISO 14031 guidelines are aimed at all organizations regardless of type, size, location and complexity. The process involves three stages, namely: planning, evaluation, and review and improvement, emphasizing the importance of management commitment (see Figure 4.5).

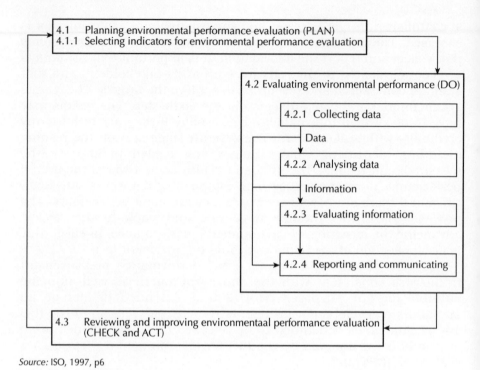

Source: ISO, 1997, p6

Figure 4.5 *Environmental Performance Evaluation*

The planning stage involves:

- Management considerations, ie organizational structure, strategy and policy, legal framework, interested parties, cultural and social factors, and resources.
- Environmental aspects.
- Selecting environmental performance indicators (EPIs) in evaluation areas and criteria.

The evaluating stage involves:

- Collecting data.
- Analysing data.
- Evaluating information.
- Reporting and communication.

The third stage involves reviewing and improving the previous two stages.

The different evaluation areas, which can help the selection of indicators, are:

- The management system, which includes people, practices and procedures at all levels of an organization, and their decisions and activities.
- The operational system, which includes the organization's physical facilities and equipment, their design and operation, and the material and energy flows used to produce and provide the organization's products and services.
- The environment, which includes air, water, land, plant and animal life, human health and natural resources.

This ISO framework is aimed at organizations to self-implement and to tailor the evaluation process to their own activities through the selection and use of appropriate performance evaluation (see below).

PERFORMANCE EVALUATION AND STAKEHOLDER INVOLVEMENT

In this chapter we do not propose to outline detailed performance indicators. These may be possible at the industrial level, but the framework we will use eventually will be based on companies themselves having a detailed and transparent policy, and reporting the system to demonstrate moves towards practices which are consistent with sustainable development. At the industrial level, nevertheless, there may be some useful benchmarks which firms and their stakeholders could agree on. It is for people working in particular sectors to research and advocate the most appropriate measures for moves which are consistent with sustainable development. However, the literature which we have reviewed places much emphasis on stakeholder involvement and there is a need to consider the process by which stakeholders can be involved in the process of sustainable development performance evaluation, which is consistent with the measurement framework outlined above.

Here we propose an approach which is consistent with a social audit approach outlined by Jones and Welford (Welford, 1997). However, we will refer to it as a sustainable development dialogue since our aim is to evaluate firm level responses which are consistent with sustainable development, and at the same time, to engage stakeholders in a process by which such performance can be improved. The rationale behind this approach is to acknowledge the rights of information to a wide constituency. Firms engaging in a sustainable development dialogue would be conceived of as lying at the centre of a network of social relationships which are articulated in a manner akin to a stakeholder model. Put another way, social auditing recognizes the concepts of stewardship and accountability, and this in turn acknowledges that the whole of society has rights to information about actions taken on its behalf (eg by businesses). Thus, the sustainable development dialogue process allows the business to engage with its stakeholders (representing, in part, societal interests), listen to and respond to their views and, where necessary, explain and justify its actions. But it is not only a one-way flow. Businesses are also able to influence their stakeholders so that the ultimate outcome is derived from consensus.

The main point to stress is the importance to any sustainable development dialogue of an overarching and explicit values framework written in terms of corporate values, visions, aims and objectives. This is important because it provides the basic parameters for the ongoing dialogue between the various stakeholders and management. An explicit values framework avoids the anarchic flaws of this type of 'accounting receptivity'. In other words, it avoids a business degenerating into an unmanageable scramble of values, multiple aims and multiple measures of performance. In this way a firm can provide a sustainable development direction to its activities. Therefore, in order to measure the organization's sustainable development performance, not only is stakeholder performance measured against core values, but also company performance is measured against stakeholder values. Figure 4.6 represents a stakeholder consultation model. It shows the two-way flow of learning and accountability which are necessary to realize fully the virtues of a pluralistic strategy. The company reports to and learns from the stakeholder and the stakeholder is invited to assess the organization's performance and aspirations. The company is also able to influence the stakeholder, particularly where its own aspirations may be higher than some of its stakeholders'.

The sustainable development dialogue is operationalized through the three assessment loops depicted in Figure 4.6. At the centre of the assessment process are the core values of the organization, made explicit in the organization's values framework which is published and made widely available. The extent to which the organization is perceived to be adhering to these core values is determined through consultation with a range of stakeholders and (often key) informants (expert opinion, publicly recognized figures, etc). Where company performance is perceived to be poor, it will be either because that action really is poor or because the organization has not communicated its performance accurately or effectively. In either case, action to improve performance (or its communication) will have to be taken. Such action may require some alteration of the organization's values framework. This process is represented by Loop 1.

At the same time, the organization compares its own core values with those of its stakeholders (Loop 2). The process is firstly to define its stakeholders' values (again through consultation) and then to

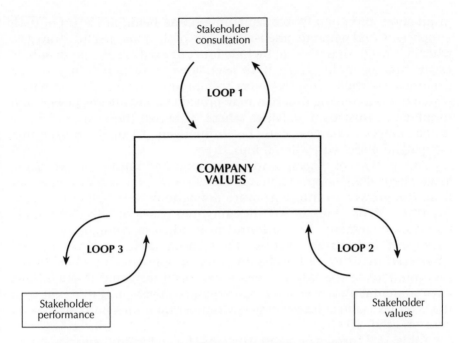

Figure 4.6 *The Sustainable Development Dialogue Process*

compare the organization's performance against these stakeholder values. Where necessary (because gaps or deficiencies are identified), core values can be reassessed and the values framework rewritten to reflect this.

The third loop involves action to influence stakeholders through the assessment of stakeholder performance against core values. Here we may find the situation where the organization considers its values to be superior to those of its stakeholders. Through education and campaigning initiatives, the organization takes action to influence stakeholders. Thus, stakeholders influence the organization through their perceptions of company performance based on its own values (Loop 1) and through an assessment of performance based on stakeholders' own values (Loop 2). The organization, in turn, tries to influence stakeholders through an assessment of stakeholder performance against its own core values (Loop 3).

SUPPLY CHAIN MANAGEMENT

A number of the models referred to in this chapter considered that there was a need for life-cycle assessment and supply chain management. We also recognized the need to see sustainable production and sustainable consumption as being made up of both supply side and demand side issues. One of the most useful strategies which we need, therefore, to include into our analysis is that of supply chain management. Here it is seen as the responsibility of the producer (service provider) both to manage downstream activities where the purchasing function may provide for significant power, and to influence upstream activities where, although there will not be so much power, choices can be influenced through marketing, campaigning and educational initiatives.

The notion of social and environmental improvement being 'negotiated' along supply chains is therefore very important and arises from the growth in intercorporate dialogue on a range of different priorities. Reflections of well-documented cases of effective supply chain management can be found in studies of companies from a variety of industrial sectors. Joint promotional activity by the Chartered Institute of Purchasing and Supply and Business in the Environment in the last few years has been designed to encourage environmental awareness among corporate buyers and to assist with the complex issue of integrating environmental issues into purchasing (Morton et al, 1997).

Table 4.7 provides good reasons for adopting supply chain management techniques and provides guidance for the introduction of environmental aspects into purchasing power. However, our aim would be to extend such techniques to cover both the social and ethical aspects of sustainable development, and to put more emphasis on the management and influence of demand for the product or service in question.

A CONCEPTUAL FRAMEWORK FOR SUSTAINABLE PRODUCTION AND SUSTAINABLE CONSUMPTION

The basic framework we chose to adopt is based on the six Es approach advocated in the previous chapter and summarized above. This is because it encompasses so many of the elements advocated by others who present frameworks of environmental management and sustainable development at the firm level. However, we extend this framework in two ways. Firstly, although Welford (1997) sees the importance of employment within the economy measure presented in his framework, a number of commentators see this as so fundamental to a move towards practices which are consistent with sustainable development that we add it to the list of areas under consideration in terms of a seventh 'E'. Secondly, and more fundamentally, the framework developed by Welford (1997) might be seen as somewhat static and many commentators make reference to the need for a more

Table 4.7 *Principles of Buying into the Environment*

1 Understand the business reasons	Examine the implications of legislation, market opportunities and pressures, supply chain risk, community needs
2 Know your environment	Understand: environmental responsibilities, policies and issues, improvement targets and programmes
3 Understand your supply chain	Rank key suppliers based on environmental issues and risks. Develop environmental purchasing policy and processes
4 Adopt a partnership style	Communicate openly and clearly. Explore areas of cooperation for mutual benefits
5 Collect only information needed	Identify key questions and define information needs. Select suitable collection methods
6 Validate supplier's performance	Select, where necessary, a suitable method to validate information and management systems
7 Set a timetable for improvement	Discuss and agree improvement targets with environmental managers and suppliers

Source: Green, Morton and New, 1996

dynamic model which is consistent with product stewardship and life-cycle assessment. We introduce, therefore, supply chain management into the model.

This is done by recognizing that sustainable production and consumption is made up of supply side issues and demand side issues. In managing sustainable production, therefore, we need to consider not only the practices of the firm under consideration, but also their activities in putting pressure on other firms further down the supply chain. We call this supplier pressure. Equally, in influencing sustainable consumption it is important to influence choice and to manage provision. Here the use of words is important. Since it is not possible to manage entirely the services which consumers demand, the best the form can do is to influence that choice. However, in terms of service provision, the firm is more able to manage the process because ownership of a service is rarely transferred. This approach is summarized in Table 4.8.

As a starting point, the company should be clear about its commitment to each of the 28 areas defined in the matrix above. In

Table 4.8 *A Framework for Sustainable Production and Consumption in the Service Sector*

	Sustainable production and consumption			
	Supply side issues Managing sustainable production		Demand side issues Influencing sustainable consumption	
	Supplier pressure	Own practices	Influencing choice	Managing provision
Environment				
Employment				
Economics				
Empowerment				
Ethics				
Equity				
Education				

effect this is what we referred to earlier as the vision of the company, which should be made explicit through the publication of a policy.

The operationalization of the framework should be based on three stages, namely: planning, evaluation and review. It should be consistent with the approach taken by James and Bennett (1994) and should follow the stages outlined below.

Planning

- Define the environmental context in terms of the objectives which are consistent with moves towards sustainable development in the 28 areas identified in Table 4.8.
- Consider the appropriate potential measures, including priority areas, for the industry under consideration.
- Select the measures by their appropriateness to their purpose, cost effectiveness, comparability and compatibility with other measures.

Evaluation

- Evaluate the current position.
- Implement the measures through systems that collect and report the information and communicate these to the relevant staff and stakeholders.

- Monitor results, verify results and communicate these in an appropriate way to ensure credibility with stakeholders.
- Act on the results, including identifying what changes are needed to improve the measures and results.

Review

- Review the overall performance measurement system, establishing if it works satisfactorily and if there are new areas where measurement is necessary.
- The process should then continue, starting again at stage one, aiming for continual improvement.

At the same time such a measurement framework should be defined and reported upon to allow for the sustainable development dialogue advocated above. This means seeing the policy as being central to the vision of the company and using this and the results of the evaluation stage above to create meaningful dialogue with stakeholders.

As Gray (1994) argues, the impact of this information on this constituency and their associated response can be assumed to encourage the new practices which are necessary for sustainable development. If accountability and transparency are embraced, then the corporation will find itself more closely in tune with its wider constituents and the company will develop its culture from a recognition of different stakeholder expectations and needs. But this is by no means an easy process. There will be trade-offs that have to be made if sustainability is to be pursued.

CONCLUSIONS

Moving towards business practices which are consistent with the attainment of sustainable development is a huge challenge. In many ways it represents such a fundamental change in the values and visions of companies that it cannot be expected to occur quickly. Nevertheless, as firms and their stakeholders see that the challenge of sustainable development is fundamental to the survival of the planet, so we will see more efforts being placed on procedures which can reflect the needs which are inherent in such a challenge.

As businesses do accept the need to plan their operations in line with the principles of sustainable development, so they will look for useful frameworks which they can adopt. In this chapter we have proposed one such framework, derived from the literature on corporate environmental performance and sustainable development strategies. We have provided three things. Firstly, a framework for building a vision of sustainable development at the corporate level which integrates supply chain management to reflect the need for both sustainable production and sustainable consumption. Secondly, we advocate a measurement framework based on the idea of continuous improvement. Thirdly, we define a process of sustainable development dialogue which involves two-way communications between firms and their stakeholders.

There is still much to do, however. The framework needs to be trailed by different firms in different sectors. This will almost certainly lead to some refinements being made in the approach. The framework needs to be used to define certain benchmarks or minimum standards at the industrial level. Last, but not least, the framework needs to be used in such a way that it creates transparency and openness between a firm and its stakeholders so that real dialogue can map out a workable and effective transition towards business practices which are more consistent with sustainable development. As a conceptual model that is potentially able to deliver these advantages, we believe that it can make a significant contribution.

Chapter 5

Towards Sustainable Marketing

INTRODUCTION

No company can be a sustainable company unless it is successful. That means that it has to achieve its traditional business objectives as well as to try its best to act in a way which is consistent with sustainable development. For many people there may appear to be a number of conflicts here. It is often assumed that being socially and environmentally sensitive will cost money. However, we have seen many case studies of companies where this is not the case. But even where operationalizing sustainable development in the business organization does add to costs, this is still consistent with good business, so long as the benefits of differentiating the company and its products in that way exceed the costs. Therefore, what is very important for a company that wants to move in the direction of sustainable development is the ability to differentiate its products and its overall corporate image. Therefore, the marketing function is vital if the organization is to communicate its difference. However, there is a clear win-win situation here if, at the same time as communicating the difference, the company can also persuade and educate its consumers and the wider public to act in more environmentally friendly and socially responsible ways.

This chapter therefore examines the role of the company in persuading its consumers to act in ways which are consistent with sustainable development, while at the same time making sure that its own profile is both environmentally and socially responsible. In the past, marketing, and particularly the concept of 'green marketing', may have been identified as a barrier towards creating a sustainable society, but here it is demonstrated that there is, in fact, great potential in using marketing tools to persuade and educate the consumer and to campaign for a more sustainable society.

Traditionally, the concept of 'green marketing' often seems to be one associated more with hype and overzealous claims about a product's environmental impact than with anything positive that gives consumers full information about their products. It has had a history associated with false claims, misleading statements about environmental 'credentials', and has led to a situation where many consumers simply do not believe some of the claims associated with greener products. In many ways this has caused problems for those companies which are genuinely trying to differentiate their products based on some sort of environmental profile. It means that companies must not only convince consumers of the validity of their product claims but must also become associated with having an environmentally sound corporate image. Thus in this chapter, green marketing is considered widely to encompass both products and company profiles and is also linked closely with other aspects of a company's efforts to promote sustainable development, particularly in the areas of education and campaigning.

Of course, the concept of marketing is not new, emerging as it did in the early part of the 1900s in response to changes in the economic and competitive marketplace. New mass production techniques increased the supply of goods to the point where they overtook demand, and therefore producers had to find ways of selling their goods and keep their mass production systems at full capacity (Peattie, 1992). In other words, producers had to create markets for their products and they did this by creating desires on the part of an increasingly wealthy population. Mass-production processes tended initially to reduce the price of standardized products, but businesses soon began to see the need to differentiate themselves from their competitors and matching their product ranges to their customers' perceived needs.

Many definitions of marketing exist. They include those which are expressly concerned with ensuring that consumers get what they want: 'Marketing is a social process by which individuals and groups obtain what they need and want through creating and exchanging products and values with others' (Kotler, 1984, p4), and extend to those which are all-embracing: 'Marketing is so basic that it cannot be considered a separate function... It is the whole business seen from the customer's point of view' (Drucker, 1973, p6). Because the concept of sustainable development requires us to take a holistic view of business, marketing is seen as akin to 'total management', embracing a wide array of disciplines from the inception and creation of new products, cost management and the pricing of goods, through logistics management and on to promotion, sales and after-service, which is the front line between the firm and its customers. But it also embraces the overall profile of the company, its reputation, corporate image, sponsorship, education programmes and campaigning activities. Indeed, if used ethically and effectively, it is argued here that green marketing can make a significant contribution to moving us down the path towards sustainable development. Because businesses are so powerful and because retailers, in particular, have such close contact with individuals, there is a significant contribution for the business world to make in this sort of process.

Marketing is dependent on the structures, processes and systems within which the firm operates. This includes the competitive, economic, political, social and cultural spheres to which the marketing strategy has to be matched. To many, therefore, green marketing is a simple and natural extension of the marketing process, recognizing the importance of environmental and ecological considerations at every level of the organization and in the marketplace. It is argued here, however, that rather than an extension to traditional marketing (which is too often associated simply with getting people to buy more), green marketing represents a discontinuous shift in corporate philosophy (which ought to be associated with people buying better). Green marketing ought to be ethical, ecological and compatible with sustainable development. In part it represents a culture change process which emphasizes cooperation rather than competition, eliminates sales hype and provides honest information to the consumer. Its selling techniques are non-stereotypical, non-exploitative and open to public scrutiny. Marketing, as considered here, stresses education and points to the need for both social and environmental responsibility on the part of both producers and consumers.

The context in which the business operates has been changed because of a growing public familiarity with environmental issues. This is likely to continue, and the consumer is going to be more and more sophisticated in his or her choices and in what he or she believes from the corporate message. The next decade will also see people embracing a range of social issues, and the marketing function of the business will have to respond to this as well. It is likely that people will become less trusting of companies, and indeed catastrophes such as the *Exxon Valdez* oil spill, the Chernobyl incident and Bhopal only highlight to consumers that much of the world's ecological destruction has been caused directly by the drive towards more and more output without regard to ecological protection and safety.

This situation means that the way firms communicate with the outside world through their products, services and other activities is going to have to be more open and honest. Moreover, they will have to recognize that consumers will switch away from their products if they believe that a company is not acting in a reasonable way. Callenbach et al (1993) report that 25 per cent of American consumers claim that they have changed their buying choices because of negative impressions of particular companies. Many companies are thinking much harder about the ways they are portraying themselves and building ethical and ecological considerations into the communications strategies.

Here, the marketing function is seen therefore as a very wide one. It must encompass all the operations and activities of the firm, emphasize the social and environmental life-cycle impact of a product and look carefully at an organization's corporate image. It must be involved in setting ecological criteria for product design, it must carefully consider packaging and promotion of products, and it should be open and honest about the achievements of the firm from an ecological perspective and be able to demonstrate commitment to do even more. More than anything, it needs to give the consumer honest and accurate information about products so that better informed decisions can be made. It ought to help in that decision-making through providing education to consumers and it must take a lead in demonstrating its own commitment to sustainable development.

Advertising policies will also have to adapt to changing conditions, a more ethical approach to business and an increased distaste of stereotypical or offensive images. Advertising will have to be more specific and all claims will have to be capable of proof to overcome the chronic public scepticism resulting from traditional approaches to marketing and dishonest environmental claims. The role of advertising needs to be extended to be compatible with the educational and campaigning role of the business which is advocated in this chapter.

TRADITIONAL APPROACHES TO 'GREEN MARKETING'

Authors such as Peattie (1992) see green marketing as a new variation of traditional marketing techniques and strategies. He defines green marketing as 'the management process responsible for identifying, anticipating and satisfying the requirements of customers and society, in a profitable and sustainable way' (p11) and is seen as different from more conventional approaches in four main ways:

- it has an open-ended rather than a long-term perspective;
- it focuses more strongly on the natural environment;
- it treats the environment as something which has an intrinsic value over and above its usefulness to society; and
- it focuses on global concerns rather than on those of particular societies.

Such an approach is certainly a step forward, although if one considers it in terms of the broader concept of sustainable development, it might be seen as a somewhat marginalist type of approach. Perhaps more problematically, however, it is an approach which invites companies to pay lip-service to environmentalism because it never spells out precise ecological criteria and never requires them to demonstrate clearly their own commitment to environmental responsibility.

Other commentators (eg Coddington, 1993) go further and see green marketing as requiring two main features:

- an environmental perspective which appreciates the effect of corporate actions on the environment; and
- environmental commitment where the organization resolves to become an environmental steward and to reflect that posture in all its actions.

The elements of this approach are laid out in Figure 5.1.

Having the right perspective requires an understanding of the severity and the breadth of the environmental crisis both in relation to physical issues such as air, water and land degradation and the wider but related issues such as animal rights and species preservation. All problems must be seen to have global, national and local characteristics and the marketing strategy must identify with the issues at each of these levels. Perspective must be backed up with commitment. Such commitment must recognize the need to translate

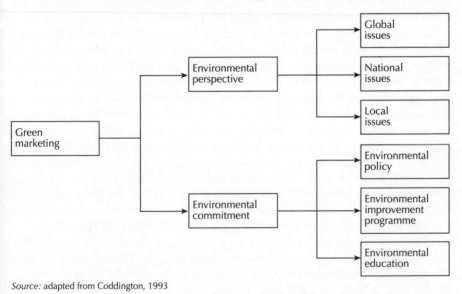

Source: adapted from Coddington, 1993

Figure 5.1 *Elements of the Green Marketing Strategy*

marketing rhetoric into reality in a proactive way. Thus, such a green marketing approach must be consistent with the aims and strategies of environmental management techniques, including the introduction of an environmental policy, an environmental improvement programme and environmental education.

MARKETING AND SUSTAINABLE DEVELOPMENT

It has been argued that marketing ought to represent a discrete shift in emphasis away from traditional approaches, putting stress on certain aspects of a product towards an ethical approach which takes a holistic view of the social and environmental aspects of the product from cradle to grave and considers the context in which it is produced. Marketing is about the provision to the consumer of information about the product and the manufacturer, along with advice on how to use the product most successfully and advice on the reuse, repair, recyclability and disposal of the product. It represents, therefore, product stewardship at its best. It aims not only to meet the needs of the consumer but considers all stakeholders. It is not only about selling, but encompasses wider issues such as environmental education and campaigning for the issues which will help to bring about sustainability.

The stakeholder concept emphasizes the need to satisfy a whole range of often disparate demands, and the role of sustainable marketing is to track these demands and to try to satisfy them where appropriate. For example, there will be demands from customers for socially and environmentally friendly products at reasonable prices with high quality attributes, demands from shareholders for profitability and dividends, and demands from employees for fair wages and job security. Where conflict between competing aims exists, it has been the stakeholders with most power (usually measured in crude financial terms) who win the battle. However, if our ultimate aim is sustainable development, all other demands must be considered as secondary to this and profit-centred strategies replaced by more holistic and integrated approaches. A starting point must be to make stakeholders aware of each other's demands in an open and honest way. This approach, which has been alien to so many organizations in the past, must be part of an organization's corporate culture if the company is to claim honestly that it is seeking to improve the whole of its social and environmental performance.

The most important lesson to be learned from the stakeholder concept is that cooperation is as important as competition. Trust relations have to be developed with stakeholders and this is best built up by honesty and openness. Companies which are serious about improving their social and environmental performance should have nothing to hide and therefore the disclosure of as much information as possible, without giving away competitive advantages, is central to a sustainable strategy. Therefore, both product specific information and company profiling in 'sustainable development reports' is crucial if the consumer is to make a decision regarding both the product which is bought and from whom it is bought. A preference for buying products from companies which can exhibit a positive social and environmental image is likely to be a characteristic of consumer preferences in the future.

Although social and environmental considerations are increasingly important to the consumer, such attributes alone will be insufficient to sell a product. Not only must the product recognize traditional market requirements (ie it must be fit for the purpose for which it was intended, have the desired quality and delivery attributes, and be price competitive), it must also consider its profile and the profile of its producer with regard to wider ecological issues such as worker rights, the treatment of women and minority groups, animal testing and any impact on developing countries and indigenous populations. In other words, the company must be capable of responding to a whole range of issues which are consistent with sustainable development. Failure to meet these basic requirements will result ultimately in the failure of the product.

Marketing cannot be looked at in isolation, however. The effects of launching a new product or reorienting an existing one to have superior social and environmental attributes will have ramifications for procurement, finance, human resources, production processes and delivery. The fundamental key to a green marketing strategy is to approach the problem in a systematic way, undertaking thorough research and planning. Consideration of longer timescales for activities will also be important. But sustainable marketing requires the company even to reconsider some of the basic assumptions about doing business. For example, it may not be consistent with sustainable development if the company continues to try to persuade the consumer simply to buy more and more. An education process, teaching the consumer to buy less, may actually be more appropriate. While this might be seen as bad business at first, the experience of companies such as Dow Chemicals, which has educated farmers to purchase fewer fertilizers, has shown that rather than lose its customers, they have actually gained their trust so that their business is retained and overall sales actually increase at the expense of other less enlightened companies.

The way in which a company improves its social and environmental performance will depend in part on its functional organization, its geographical spread and its markets. Ultimately though, the organization must make the sustainable development a priority.

Within the marketing mix there are a number of priorities that need to be addressed, and the following checklist identifies these:

1   *Corporate Policy*
    Marketing is as much about marketing the organization as any of its products. It is no good producing a product with superior social and environmental attributes if the very nature of the firm in which it is produced leads to development paths which are unsustainable. There is therefore a need to ensure that the organization has in place appropriate management strategies and that it is committed to moving towards sustainable development.
2   *Product Policy*
    Products should be designed with sustainable development in mind. In particular they should minimize the use of non-renewable resources and be designed for disassembly and recyclability. They should ensure that they are produced in a responsible way and that procurement policies are non-exploitative. Products with clear social and environmental attributes can be labelled as such, but it is important not to overstate or be dishonest about these aspects of the product. More importantly, an educational process or product stewardship approach should accompany the sale of the product, ensuring that the customer uses the product as it is intended.
3   *Packaging*
    Packaging should be designed which, while fit for its purpose, uses the minimum amount of materials. Use should be made of packaging materials which minimize damage to the environment and the company should arrange for packaging to be recycled or taken back and where possible reused. Excess packaging used as promotional material is unethical and not in the spirit of sustainable development.
4   *Promotion Policy*
    Promotions should highlight the social and environmental credentials of both the organization and its products or services. The reputation of the firm may be enhanced by public relations and advertising exercises, but all claims must be credible, honest and true. Moreover, promotions should merge with education and campaigning so that organizations are involved in broadly based strategies to improve the environment and to move towards sustainable development.
5   *Pricing Policy*
    If social and environmental protection measures cost extra money, this can be passed on to the consumer, making it clear that the price differential is a result of such improvements. If costs are reduced through environmental measures, it is ethical to be

completely honest in cutting prices or considering discounts to those who can match the organization's own environmental performance. It is often said that price is an indicator of quality; in the future we may also see price as an indicator of socially and environmentally responsible business. Consumers need to be educated to realize that paying a little more for a product (where necessary) is very much a price worth paying.

6   *Transportation and Distribution*

Preference should be given to transportation systems which have reduced environmental costs in terms of energy consumption and pollution (widely defined). Where appropriate, distribution channels should be established between the producer, wholesalers, retailers and customers which minimize transportation and packaging needs. These same systems can also be used to ensure that used products and packaging are recycled. The distribution system can also be seen as a process by which information about products and profiles of businesses can be transmitted. They can be used effectively as a conduit for education and campaigning.

7   *Quality and Effectiveness*

Quality is part of the environmental profile of a product. Quality goods last longer, break down less frequently, are worth repairing and often use less energy. It is important that any environmental attributes do not detract from quality or the effectiveness of the product. If this is not possible, then that fact should be explained clearly to the consumer. But good quality can also be widely defined to include both positive environmental and social attributes. If, for example, one views environmental degradation or human exploitation as a quality defect, then good management requires a move away from quantity and towards quality.

8   *Personnel Policy*

Commitment is at the heart of a proactive strategy for sustainable development and it is important to ensure that the whole workforce is sensitive to social and environmental issues and understands how to ensure improvement which is consistent with sustainable development. Awareness of the importance of sustainable development should be enhanced by training and education, and there should be employee reward schemes which are consistent with meeting the stated aims of the company, including the social and environmental performance of the organization.

9   *Information systems*

The organization must ensure that there is an adequate monitoring system which is capable of identifying potential and real social and environmental problems. Suppliers must be made aware of corporate requirements and must have their own strategies which are consistent with the organization's policy of moving towards a situation which is consistent with sustainable development. The organization must collect and collate relevant information so that it can be responsive and report to stakeholders.

10 *Education, Communications and Product Stewardship*
Linked closely with the information system, there must be a clear strategy for communications with consumers, which will include education about the product they are using and how to use it more effectively, advice on what to do after the product has been used and an element of wider education and campaigning in the context of sustainable development. Companies are likely to produce regular reports on the social and environmental profile of their activities, and to set out aims and objectives for the future.

While the ten elements of a sustainable marketing strategy outlined above will move the organization towards a strategy which is more consistent with sustainable development, it must be remembered that the marketing function does not exist in isolation and that no positive claims should be made unless they can be justified and verified. Fundamental to the marketing function will be the collection and management of information and a clear role for education and communication. These are issues which we need to deal with in more depth.

INFORMATION AND REPORTING FOR SUSTAINABLE DEVELOPMENT

Central to any sustainable marketing strategy will be the identification of new issues, market trends and the state of scientific knowledge and technology. Market research and accurate information will be needed on which to build successful campaigns. Marketing requires information to be effective, and therefore sustainable marketing is nothing without accurate information on the social and environmental impact of both the company and its competitors. A continuous flow of information and data is needed on both processes and products, and central to this will be life-cycle analysis, social and environmental audits and dialogue with stakeholders. These need to be on-going activities that produce information relating to the overall performance and social and environmental conduct of the whole organization. However, information is often collected in a rather haphazard way which leads to a narrow and piecemeal focus. There is therefore a need for some sort of system whereby information is collected and collated in a planned and productive way and from which reports are produced and published. The aim of such a system must be to enable managers to make more effective decisions, to act as a database for answering queries from stakeholders and to aid in education and campaigning initiatives.

The first consideration is where to find relevant information. Here it is useful to group sources into three categories: primary sources, secondary sources and cooperative alliances. Let us deal with each in turn.

Primary sources

Primary information is very much about direct research. It means collecting information which is based on surveys of one sort or another. Large quantitative surveys based on questionnaires can elicit interesting information about overall market trends and changing consumer attitudes. Just as valuable, however, are more qualitative techniques which are associated, for example, with focus groups. Focus groups will often be useful in testing the results of large surveys. For example, we know that quantitative research suffers from the so-called halo effect – ie many interviewees want to appear more virtuous than they actually are. A more informal approach to the collection of data through the focus group can often elicit more truthful information.

Secondary sources

Secondary materials include trade and industry association publications, specialist journals, consumer magazines, professional association materials, annual books and reviews, and specialist market surveys. These secondary sources are relatively cheap, although they do not provide, of course, the specific focus which an individual firm may require. They do create, however, a useful reference library and provide general information on market trends and attitudes. Market studies in particular, however, often provide a great deal of very detailed research and sometimes produce forecasts of market and consumer trends. More market studies with a green focus are likely to be published as demand for them grows among businesses.

Cooperative alliances

An important (often overlooked) means of gathering information is through cooperative alliances with other organizations. Alliances with other firms, NGOs and government agencies to collect general information will be cost effective and informative. Arrangements with local pressure groups, universities, government agencies and other interest groups can all provide marketing managers with extra eyes and ears and different perspectives on social and environmental information. It is possible to establish think-tanks made up of groups of people with diverse interests and specialities, and this will often provide an in-depth, unbiased approach to public policy research which is simply not possible using any other source. The outcomes of these sorts of exercises (often used in association with primary and secondary research) are often of extremely high quality.

We can also consider social and environmental information as broadly falling into three categories. Figure 5.2 maps out an environmental information system where we have categorized information into stakeholder information, impact information and scientific information. This all feeds into a central data collection function and library. Let us deal with each type of information in turn.

Stakeholder information

The challenge facing the modern socially and environmentally aware enterprise is to satisfy the many (often disparate) demands of a whole range of stakeholders. It is important, therefore, to monitor these demands through systems that collect information from employees, customers, shareholders, local communities and others. Each of these stakeholders brings a different dimension to the organization. The organization's sustainable development policy and stakeholders' reactions to that and the associated management system will be one strand which pulls together information. Other information is likely to be more primary information about consumer attitudes, pressure group activities and regulators' reactions.

Impact information

Central to any open, honest and credible marketing policy will be a need to understand and have information about the social and environmental impact of the organization's operations and processes. Again, there will be two distinct streams of information. On a continuous basis there should be monitoring of all inputs to the organization and all outputs (including discharges, emissions and other pollution) from the organization. There should be a periodic consolidation to check that there are no hidden wastes or discharges. Secondly, the marketing function should be able to draw on periodic social and environmental audit reports and full life-cycle assessments of all its products. Life-cycle assessment and product stewardship strategies in particular will be central to any marketing campaign.

Technical information

Technical issues play a prominent role in virtually every aspect of the organization's environmental strategy. It is important, for example, to have knowledge of the best available techniques and the best available technologies, since in most countries this is required by law either implicitly or explicitly. Secondly, to be proactive there is a need to collect information on the legal and regulatory stance of governments, and on general societal expectations with regard to both the environment and social responsibility.

We can see from Figure 5.2 that all this information, held together in a reference library, should give us a picture of market conditions and opportunities, and will be used to formulate marketing objectives and a marketing strategy. Ultimately those objectives and that strategy should be consistent with the aims of sustainable development through ecological management techniques and strategies which are consistent with sustainability. Once the sustainable marketing strategy has been defined, it should be matched with consistent education and campaigning initiatives and result in periodic reports on the company's progress towards running its business in a way which is consistent with sustainable development.

COMMUNICATING THE DIFFERENCE

Communications will be a key element in any marketing process. Accurate information about products and the wider social and environmental aspects of processes should be communicated to all stakeholders and particularly customers. In particular, at the centre of the sustainable marketing process should be a product stewardship approach whereby advice and help about the use and disposal of the product should be given to all those who will come into contact with it after it has left the factory gates. There is, of course, no magic method or style of promotion and information provision. Essentially, explaining the attributes of an environmentally friendlier and socially responsible product should be approached in just the same way as any other communication message. The central message should always be visible, understood, relevant and honest. The company should be prepared to prove what has been said and be open to further questions about its overall social and environmental profile.

Companies which are promoting an environmentally friendly image will have to be very precise about what they say and truly

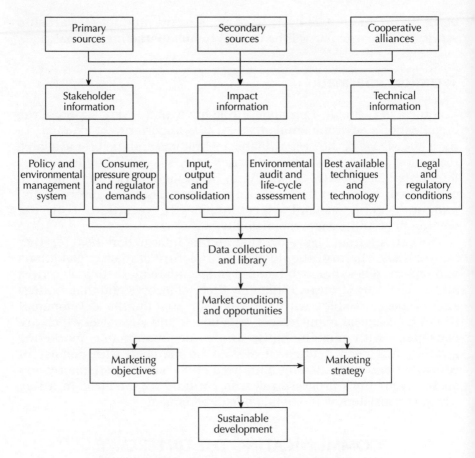

Figure 5.2 *Environmental Information System*

practise what they preach. Drawing attention to the environmental aspects of a business will draw attention increasingly from a more sceptical public and better informed media. If there is something about a product or organization worth communicating, then the key question must be to whom do you communicate. Undoubtedly, the first group to concentrate on are the consumers of the product.

However, the sustainable development message may be rather more difficult to communicate than many consumer surveys of consumer attitudes might suggest. We have already argued that the halo effect promotes rhetoric and obscures reality. While theoretically willing to buy alternative products, we know that most consumers, in practice, are not happy about giving up the brands they know and the price, quality and performance standards they have come to expect, especially for alternative, more uncertain purchases which might actually be at a higher price. One of the problems is that past marketing campaigns with respect to greener products have made situations worse by being deceitful. Many consumers have become confused, cynical and disillusioned with many green products. Companies cannot jump to conclusions, therefore, about consumers' understanding of, and their likelihood to respond to, green communications. Moreover, when one tries also to explain a product's socially responsible profile, one is left with even bigger dilemmas. There is, therefore, a need to look very closely at markets and consumer behaviour before effective communications can be developed. In the main, the onus will be on the marketers to educate consumers, to simplify social and environmental issues (without decreasing their importance) and then to offer product solutions. Marketers should also think about the profile of the company as a whole, though, and consider campaigning strategies which are consistent with this profile.

The consumer will also be affected indirectly through the behaviour of competitors and through the media, politicians and a range of pressure groups. There are, therefore, many other key targets for any communications. Increasingly, business-to-business communication is becoming more and more important for manufacturers and suppliers. If a company (and particularly a retailer) is developing its social and environmental stance, it is going to be more demanding of the social and environmental practices of its suppliers.

The first consideration concerning communication is often not what to say about your company or product, but whether there is anything to say at all. There are two concerns here. Firstly, communicating a less-than-thorough or dubious social or environmental initiative runs the risk of alienating consumers and opinion formers if there are gaps in the message, inaccuracies in the claims or secrets in the organization. In overstating claims, negative regulatory, pressure group and media responses could endanger the product, service or corporate integrity. Bad publicity could negate everything the company was trying to achieve and would certainly act against any positive corporate image which a company was trying to foster. Secondly, there is an issue concerning whether a certain message is appropriate to consumers at all. The impact of the message will depend on how aware, committed and educated the consumers of a product are and on the particular market characteristics in which the product is sold. In the first instance, a company needs to establish whether social and environmental considerations are or could be significant in their markets and whether appropriate messages could confer a competitive advantage.

There are a number of communications techniques that can be used to get the message across. However, in order to be effective it is important that, whichever methods are chosen, they are used within an integrated and coordinated strategy of moving towards a situation which is consistent with sustainable development. Even now, consumers are still swamped with the clichéd, generic imagery of greening in environmental messages: rainbows, trees, plants, green fields, dolphins and smiley planets. At the other end of the scale, far too many messages have assumed detailed consumer knowledge across the range of environmental issues. There is a need to explain each issue where appropriate and then stress the reason why the consumer should prefer one particular product over a competitors' products. When it comes to profiling the social responsibility of products, the problems are even more apparent since social issues are less well defined and may be more difficult to communicate. Nevertheless, the creative skills of marketers can produce a difference and are capable of differentiating products which are based on elements of sustainable development. It requires hard work and some experimentation, but is nevertheless vital if businesses are to help to promote the importance of sustainable development.

In terms of executing communication, companies should not over-assume people's knowledge or altruism when it comes to any social or environmental issues. Neither should they under-assume how much consumers like their current brands and labels. The majority of consumers will not be impressed with complicated explanations of why one product is more socially responsible or environmentally friendly than another. Those communicating the difference need to find simple and honest messages about why one product should be preferred. Perhaps most importantly, however, the company needs to create a positive profile of itself and all its activities in order to gain the trust of consumers and help to add credibility to any specific product claims made.

Communications through the medium of advertising are likely to form a part of any marketing strategy. However, we have already suggested that clichéd imagery and stereotypical role models are hardly consistent with a move towards strategies which are consistent with sustainable development. Sexist, racist and homophobic categorizations of people are more likely to cause offence to educated consumers than to convince them to buy a particular product or service. Moreover, the tokenism paid to minority groups which is apparent in many commercials is equally offensive and will be interpreted as a cynical attempt to appear ethical.

It is often clear what should be avoided in advertising campaigns but less clear what is effective and consistent with sustainable development strategies. Callenbach et al (1993) suggest five aspects which product advertising should stress:

• lasting buyer satisfaction rather than transient;

- lifetime costs of products rather than just initial costs;
- reliability, durability and trouble-free qualities rather than initial emotional attractiveness;
- possibilities for the reuse or recycling of products and their containers; and
- the low ecological-impact features of the manufacture, distribution, use and disposal of the products.

Communicating the social, environmental and sustainable message will be very much part of a holistic strategy. Great care has to be taken about that communications strategy, particularly in respect of advertising. Like all strategies, however, the key is to be honest, open and credible and to develop a communications strategy which is consistent with all the other aspects of corporate planning and management.

EDUCATION AND CAMPAIGNING

Perhaps more than any other institutions in the world, companies have the ability to educate many people about the important concept of sustainable development. Through education programmes with their workers, suppliers and customers they can have an impact on many more people than traditional educators can reach. Large corporations may well have literally millions of people buying their products every year and that access to people gives businesses both a significant role and a responsibility to push messages associated with moving down the path of sustainable development.

In future, businesses will also be campaigners (we have seen some evidence of this already). They will realize that there is a very thin dividing line between marketing, education and campaigning. They will see that they and their products become more attractive when they take a particular line on a popular public issue (eg genetically modified food, animal testing, human rights, fair trade, etc). Therefore, business has a huge role which it can productively play in educating its staff and customers, engaging in debate regarding sustainable development and campaigning on a range of important issues.

CONCLUSIONS

Green marketing and moves towards more sustainable marketing will be central to any business organization which is committed to social and environmental improvement. However, it must be recognized that ethical and sustainable approaches must be central to the communications function. Moreover, green marketing is more than simply about selling products; it is also about educating the consumer about better use of a product in environmental terms and being part of a wider campaign to move business towards sustainable development. Therefore, it represents a discrete shift away from the more unethical and spurious green marketing strategies so common to date. Key elements of the marketing strategy include the need to recognize and chart changing consumer trends, to have clear strategies aimed at differentiating the company's marketing mix and to have integrated and effective environmental information systems. It is not enough to promote products alone, and any organization needs to examine its overall impact on and commitment to the environment. The green company will also be a campaigning company and be committed to spreading an ethical communication message about sustainable development.

Companies which are keen to identify their more environmentally friendly products within their marketing strategy will also be aided by third-party ecolabelling schemes, based on seals of approval, which will be able to confer a recognized accreditation for a particular product. As a minimum, the assessment approach should be based on a full life-cycle assessment of a product category and there should be suitable minimum criteria laid down for the award of a label. However, the schemes which are in existence will have to take on wider ecological criteria, including fundamental human and animal rights, if they are to retain their credibility and really act as an effective tool to take us towards sustainable development. From the company's perspective it will not be enough to make minor changes to a product and call it environmentally friendly, since environmental impacts need to be assessed from cradle to grave. Increasingly, the consumers' attention will be based on corporate performance as well as individual product profiles, and therefore any strategy will have to focus on the widest possible aspects of environmental impacts. Companies which take the environment seriously therefore need to adopt a proactive green marketing strategy which is much more holistic than the narrower marketing so often employed by more traditional firms.

Chapter 6

Towards Sustainable Development: a Buddhist Path

INTRODUCTION

In my view, we are currently in a period of great transformation on our planet. In the next 50 years the human race will suffer either significant destruction through environmental or social collapse based on greed, or it will learn to return to its spiritual roots, recognize its connectedness and see the development paths of the late 20th century as the madness which they are. A move towards sustainable development requires the transformation which has already started. It is not enough to rely on technological advances, changes in management practices and education alone. Much of the damage done is linked directly to individual human greed, and this is what we now need to challenge.

The ecological crisis in which we find ourselves is therefore, in part, a manifestation of a lost spirit and a mindset that fails to recognize truth, interconnectedness and complexity. Human beings themselves, through their materialism, consumption and greed, are directly responsible for most of the unsustainable practices that we see. If there is to be a real move towards sustainable development it will not be sufficient to rely on businesses, governments and other institutions. Change will have to occur within people and particularly within those of us who live in the West.

In order to move towards a sustainable future we must go beyond seeing the environment in sterile scientific terms (with a more minor social dimension sometimes tagged on) and come to recognize, appreciate and enjoy the spiritual dimension of ecology. Of course it is vital that we reduce pollution, plant trees, clean our rivers, maintain biodiversity, recycle our products, and so on. However, we require a much more fundamental change if we are really going to reverse the destructive tendencies of the modern world. The most critical change that must take place is a transformation of our very relationship with the earth. The earth does not need to change in order to survive, but we do. We must change our values, our outlook and our behaviour. We must recognize our interconnectedness with the world.

The threatened extinction of species in the rainforests, jungles, mountains, plains, seas and rivers in the world today is the result of abrupt and violent changes wreaked on the environment by avarice and ignorance. Instead of evolving into new forms, species are simply disappearing and it is now apparent that as they disappear we will disappear with them. It is not just the destruction of food chains and ecological balance that will destroy us. When the animals are gone, our very humaneness will disappear. We do not exist without the richness of the environment around us. As we kill off one more species, then part of us is lost as well. This is all part of the spiritual dimension of ecology which we must try to regain. This chapter makes some suggestions about how we can do just that.

A spiritual force is absent in so much of Western culture. People have a sense of emptiness that they seek to fill by consuming more and looking towards the day when they might just be able to amass all those material comforts that they dream of. We become cocooned in walls of bricks and mortar that keep us secure and warm. But that cocoon often prevents us from breaking free from the day-to-day habits, pressures and norms which would then allow us to explore a wider spiritual existence. But more and more people are exploring new spiritual dimensions and are discovering simplicity and humility. Such individuals can be a great force for change as a critical mass of enlightenment builds up.

CHALLENGING SIMPLISTIC THINKING

One of the characteristics of modern society is the tendency for people to offer very simple solutions to extremely complex issues. Because of this complexity, people try to understand and explain events in ways which they can handle, and this leads to a degree of simplistic thinking on a range of issues. When you realize that racism and nationalism are products of such simplistic thinking, you can see the danger of this when it manifests itself as a justification for so-called ethnic cleansing. But simplistic thinking is also commonplace in economics, in the way we run businesses, in the determination of our own life-styles and in beliefs about what will make us happy. If we are really going to progress along a path which is more consistent with sustainable development, the first thing to challenge is such simplistic thinking.

However, simplistic thinking is often actually encouraged in society and many of its institutions, including the Church, the 'family', political parties, the mass media and senior managers of our businesses. It is convenient for the people in power to discourage more complex thinking and debate. But by discouraging thinking we discourage the inner growth which can come about through contemplation, meditation and a re-evaluation of values and beliefs.

One of the biggest lies often promoted in Western societies is the myth that 'we are here to be happy'. Such a message is promoted by those who push materialism and its associated tools of persuasion in order to associate consumption with happiness. It is a convenient and simplistic way of dealing with the real complexity and uncertainty which is really representative of the world in which we live. But it is also a view which is fundamentally damaging to the human spirit and to inner growth. We often go along with it because we are lazy, or because we are too busy getting more and more enveloped in the type of society where we have to work harder and harder to satisfy our material desires.

One example of simplistic thinking surrounds the concept of unlimited growth. Such growth is not only impossible, since resources (with the exception of solar energy) are strictly finite, but it is also fundamentally misguided. That growth is good and necessary to bring about stability, prosperity and happiness is a view taken by most governments in the world and which most economists never even question, but the growth which we have seen that is supposed to satisfy these aspirations has actually put the earth's future at risk through a reckless exploitation of natural resources. Moreover, rather than act to improve the standards of living of future generations, it has actually put them in jeopardy. Such is the selfishness of the advanced industrial economies.

Another aspect of the deluded thinking which is prevalent in most Western economies is a psychological one. People seem to believe that the pursuit of more and more money and more and more material possessions is the path towards greater happiness, satisfaction and contentment. But in many cases, no matter how wealthy people become or how high their standard of living, they often die without realizing contentment. Indeed, they often die early precisely because they are so stressed out, having engaged all their life in a 'rat race' to nowhere. Indeed, the greedier we become, the less likely we are to find happiness and contentment.

Too many people are caught up in a cycle of acquiring more and more goods. They are obsessed with the single goal of money, and this results in there being no space left in their lives for spiritual development. This is the great tragedy of our times: few people actually recognize that true contentment comes through looking at life as a whole and not concentrating on only one narrow aspect of it. Such a holistic approach is missing in most people's lives; they prefer simplistic solutions to what they perceive as simple problems. That means equating happiness and contentment with materialism, and satisfying that by grasping more and more money.

SPIRITUALITY AS A CORE VALUE

The above critique of the simplistic thinking to be found in the West is not, of course, a recipe for abandoning the whole system and returning to some sort of feudal existence. Too often people equate criticism of the present economic system as a call for returning to past values. Rather, I suggest that it is actually time to move forward, but in a direction which is radical and puts spiritual development central to people's lives and to society as a whole. This means rediscovering ancient wisdom and finding a balance in our lives, or what might be commonly called a 'middle way'. Criticizing materialism does not mean that all people must become hermits, nuns or monks. It simply means finding a balance between having the possessions we need or that are truly meaningful to us and other aspects of our lives.

There are many aspects of our lives which could be developed fruitfully: a love and appreciation of nature for its own sake, an appreciation of aesthetics, honesty and integrity, self-respect and respect for others, humility, generosity, understanding and knowledge. An emphasis on economic growth and materialism has often led to there being very little space for the development of these aspects of human existence.

We must recognize that self-esteem should come not from what we do, not from how people perceive us, but from who we really are inside. In other words, it is not external factors which give us meaning, but factors within ourselves which can provide meaning, security, value and self-worth. None of this can be based on the human ego, but can be developed only through a process of humility and inner development. We must seek balance in our lives. Of course we will make mistakes, but there are lessons to be learned from all mistakes, such that even negative experiences can turn out to be positive.

A BUDDHIST VIEW OF THE WORLD

For me, Buddhist philosophy turns the whole Western mindset, with its emphasis on the individual and the family, completely upside down for two reasons. Firstly, the Buddhist cosmology has the entire universe at its centre, in contrast to the anthropocentric worldview so commonly characterized by Western (Christian) culture. Indeed, human beings are humble in the totality and are essentially like grains of sand compared to the limitlessness of space. Secondly, the anthropocentric culture results in human beings, however well intentioned, having a self-centred and selfish approach to life. In other words, the ego comes to dominate decision-making and many humans do everything to boost this ego, trying to make themselves look more important in other people's eyes as if, in some way, that justified their existence and made their lives worthwhile. Buddhism, on the other hand, points to the ego as being the cause of much suffering and our aim, if we are to become more enlightened, should be to release this ego and concentrate on developing real humility. Indeed, humility is much more attractive to other human beings and is much more satisfying than developing a massive ego, which simply tends to alienate others.

The point about ego is that even if one attains what one desires, greater desires always emerge. The ego mindset cannot be fulfilled, and its greed for more and more satisfaction and recognition becomes the source of its own destruction. This, of course, becomes a source of suffering, because the human spirit becomes captured by the avaricious mind. The way through this life of constantly unsatisfied desires is to practise a degree of non-attachment – in other words, to develop a distance from all desires. This might sound difficult, but since the ego-mind is firmly embedded within our socialization process and since it is reinforced by Western culture and economics, it is difficult to overcome. Non-attachment should not be confused, however, with complacency. Buddhism has long taught the importance of self-control by stressing that one should judge when one has had enough of something by choosing a path of moderation rather than maximization. This will actually be more beneficial both to the self and to others.

Of course, this is just the first step for someone following the Buddhist path. The path to enlightenment is much more difficult, but one thing is certain; it is not based on attachment to material possessions and situations, rather it involves release and freedom from a destructive cycle of consumption and destruction. A concentration on contentment, rather than some individual utility optimizing process, is a good start.

Another important realization is that all forms of life are interdependent and their existence is inextricably linked to the lives of everything else. Therefore, when we harm other life we harm ourselves and when we create an environment which will no longer support certain living things or certain ways of life, we are cutting off a whole range of development paths which we have no right at all to interfere with. The web of life includes human beings because they are one element in the whole. However, we have no right to interfere with that whole, whether it is through pollution-causing activities, genetic modification or nationalistic genocide (the greatest evil of our time and something which no other species has ever engaged in).

The more common anthropocentric approach taken by human beings both impacts upon and is reinforced by the economic system which we create. The origin of economic activity derives from the basic idea that humans will always want to maximize some notion of utility which will involve the consumption of more and more resources. Implicit in such an approach is the assumption that humans have superiority over all other life forms and that they are capable of being independent of those life forms. In other words, although we rely on nature for our sustenance, we act in a way that treats nature as an object for our use (and abuse). Rather than develop a cooperative community spirit (which can be found in some agrarian Buddhist cultures), we prefer to develop systems which are capable of satisfying the needs and desires of individuals without any recourse to the impact which that can have on others and on the environment as a whole. We prefer to maximize agricultural output, for example, by using fertilizers and pesticides rather than developing methods of farming whereby crops are grown in a way which is sympathetic to, and respectful of, local conditions and local needs.

TOWARDS A NEW BUDDHIST ECONOMICS

I have proposed that Buddhism can be the source of greater individual contentment and satisfaction and that this can be more consistent with the protection of nature and care of the environment. However, such personal development paths are always going to collide with a capitalist system which pays little respect to satisfying anything but traditional anthropocentric goals. Therefore, we need to look also towards a change in the system, which seems to promote environmental destruction rather than protect it for future generations. I will not argue here that there is just one approach – that would be too simplistic. There will be many approaches and none of us can be sure which will be the most effective. However, what we can be quite sure about is the need to move away from mass consumption economies towards a more environmentally restorative economy, and here lessons from Buddhism can help us to find some solutions.

However, modern economics has become increasingly a branch of science, which has given it both a prominence and a certain direction which may not be appropriate. Since the Renaissance, science has grown into a modern religion that is seen as being capable of giving validity to objects that can be seen and measured. In the field of economics this has manifested itself in the use of quantitative methods to measure things which are concrete, making predictions about the future and otherwise refuting any other approach which would be then regarded as normative and inaccurate. Indeed, we seem actually to prefer the simplistic view of an economy that statistics and models can provide rather than engage in the complexities and diversities of the actual economic situation of a society.

The first thing to make clear, though, is that Buddhist economics will always be in conflict with the more scientific approaches to economics. In particular, the modern emphasis on neoclassical economics and its rational, optimization models are entirely at odds with the Buddhist approach, which puts much more emphasis on a normative approach. Much more important than following a path which maximizes the wealth of a nation or, more commonly, an élite within that nation, is a new economics based on 'what ought to be' or, more simply, 'what is right and just'. Most importantly, the economic system should serve the whole of society and protect the environment and its diversity. People should seek an economic system which is a servant, not a master.

Economics is, of course, very much connected to notions of development. However, while traditional economics emphasizes self-interest and material development, Buddhist economics stresses interconnectedness and 'inner development'. It places an emphasis also on economic approaches which were culturally appropriate. So often in the last decade (and particularly during the period of economic turmoil in South East Asia), we have seen Western economic models indiscriminately applied in inappropriate ways, causing the poor to suffer, leading to the breakdown of community values and doing little to reverse the continued environmental destruction which has been a common feature of many development paths. A Buddhist approach involves an emphasis on a much more sustainable development whereby both human beings and living creatures can realize their potential and where inner development and economic development are compatible, all within the context of a just society and healthy ecosystem.

Another interesting view about the type of economics emanating in the West and now coming to dominate the global economy is that it tends to be narrow in its focus. An emphasis on low inflation, low interest rates, growth, free international trade and globalization, and a rather smaller emphasis on full employment, human and community rights and environmental protection is not only sterile but also quite inflexible. If there were one single path down which we should push our economies, surely it would not be one which has actually caused as much suffering and destruction as the present one. Buddhist economics, on the other hand, would not advocate there being one path or one set of universally applicable rules. Instead it would stress the need for systems which are culturally sensitive, appropriate to time and place and linked to a real respect for all aspects of the world which we share. It would actually encourage the coexistence of multiple points of view and seem to find a 'middle way' to attain things which are just and equitable (not just for humans but for all living beings). It would stress the need for a moral dimension to economic activity.

Another concept at the heart of modern Western economics is the emphasis placed on competition. Competition, it is argued, will bring about situations where the cheapest possible goods are produced in the most efficient way and sold at the lowest possible prices, thus benefiting the maximum number of people and maximizing human welfare. This view, of course, is another example of simplistic thinking. To recognize that making cheap goods means paying low wages, and that economically efficient does not mean environmentally responsible in the modern context, might be just two starting points to realizing that competition may actually decrease welfare (widely defined) rather than maximize it. Indeed, the process of competition whereby people are caught up in an endless pressure to do things better and cheaper, with its modern emphasis on continuous improvement, can be a source of great stress and eventually makes people feel miserable and inconsequential. The pressure which such a process exerts on people in the workplace can make them feel alienated, deeply unhappy and depressed.

However, since we have seen very little development which has been culturally appropriate and environmentally sensitive, the process of 'internationalization' or 'globalization' which we have seen over the last three decades has, in reality, been a process of 'Westernization'. It has been sad to witness many values in developing countries which would be much more consistent with a process of sustainable development being usurped by a set of values which are more akin to Western-style consumption patterns, selfishness and spiritual impoverishment. Such an approach to economics has already had profound impacts on the world. Before it does any more irreversible damage, there is a need to engage with a Buddhist approach which would at least be more sympathetic to creating a system where environmental issues were given the place that they deserve.

Perhaps the most pervasive of all approaches to modern economics revolves around profitability, however. The common assumption is that there is a need to maximize profits or at least make a certain level of profits which will satisfy shareholders while allowing senior executives to consume what would otherwise be profits through large company perks and reward systems. Either way, profits are at the centre of most companies' aims. Profits, of course, are not to be seen as bad; they provide a vital source of money for reinvestment; they can provide just return to people who have taken risks in lending a new company money to be established, and they can be used as a stock of wealth to be used as a buffer during periods where the company may not fare so well. However, an overemphasis on profits, coupled with the emphasis on competition which has been outlined above, can in fact have very negative consequences.

The search for more and more profits in an internationally competitive environment means that any source of costs is a potential source of inefficiency. Thus, there is a tendency to try to use less labour and/or to push wages down (or to locate to cheap wage economies). If producers do stay in high wage economies, they tend to automate their production, leading to higher levels of unemployment and consequent poverty. The search for profits in a competitive marketplace therefore benefits only a small number of people and leaves many more feeling helpless, useless, unfulfilled and poor.

Another aspect of the emphasis on profits and competition is that, in practice, rather than creating greater wealth, the model constantly promotes growth, and we have seen that this often leads to periods of economic recession. The reasons for those recessions still may not be fully understood (surely if they were we would have corrected them), but we do know that with every recession, different groups of people tend to fare differently and that economic fluctuations commonly cause the most suffering to the poorest people and widen the gaps between the rich and the poor. This is true not only at the level of the nation state but is now clear at the level of the global economy as well. Inequity between people further reinforces suffering, as some people in desperate situations turn to crime and drug abuse.

Despite these consequences of the narrow type of economics which we see practised in many countries around the world, we see very few people actually challenging this general direction, which is not only unsustainable but actually, even now, fundamentally damaging. Politicians pick and choose the elements of economics which suit their purpose without thinking about the wider aspects of the consequences of growth, competition and globalization. They treat economics as if it existed in some sort of controllable vacuum (much as scientists have taught us to deal with the physical world) without any real appreciation of the full consequences of such narrow models both now and, perhaps more importantly, in the future. Of course the future is a mystery, but that does not mean that it should be discounted to such an extent that planning horizons hardly ever include future generations.

Economics should not be treated as if it exists in a vacuum. Economic theory does not emerge from, or develop in, a vacuum, but in a particular in a historical and social context. This means that dominant Western economic models are simply not applicable at all times and at all places and there needs to be a greater degree of sensitivity in applying certain ideas to situations where they are not appropriate. But economics seems to have been divorced from these contexts both in developing countries and developed countries. Moreover, the present context of a planet coming dangerously close to a series of major ecological collapses is largely being ignored.

Economics is fundamentally about the exchange of goods. That exchange can be in the interests of many people if it is done in a fair and equitable way. The reality is, of course, that it is not done in such a way and international trade is dominated by large oligopolistic trading companies whose fundamental aim is to buy goods as cheaply as possible and to sell them with the maximum amount of profit. But there is something even more exploitative in what they do. Not only do they seek to satisfy human desires but they also spend a great deal of time actually creating new desires in order to perpetuate their markets and create more growth. Many people end up buying goods which they do not need and which actually bring them very little satisfaction or pleasure.

Not everything we see in economics today is necessarily bad. Anyone claiming such a position would be guilty of the simplistic thinking which was criticized earlier. In the United Kingdom, Germany and other European countries we are seeing the emergence of a 'social market' system in which some of the limitations of a completely free market are being recognized. Such a framework emphasizes policies such as establishing social capital, underlining individual rights and responsibilities, creating a stakeholder society and decentralizing power. These trends are in the right direction if we are to create a more sustainable society because they create a situation in which it is easier for people to be part of that society and to contribute to it in a positive way. But they are far from ensuring the reversal of the environmental exploitation which we have seen to date.

There is now an opportunity to capitalize on the social market movement and to help people to understand the grave ecological picture of the earth and to move forward along a somewhat different path. Three fundamentals would be realized on this path. Firstly, the economics implemented in societies would benefit all people and not be skewed to a certain élite. Secondly, economics would be based on notions of tolerance in a diverse world and peace. Thirdly, we need an economics that can reverse ecological damage and put in place a more restorative economy. Let us examine those basic premises in a little more detail.

The economics originally advocated by Adam Smith was based on notions of 'self-benefit' which should have led to a competitive market economy benefiting everybody. In reality it has led to a system in which people are most interested in enriching themselves even if it is at the expense of others. In business we encourage managers to do everything to benefit the company and to strike deals which increase profits without any regard to the consequences on the people with whom the business is done. Similarly, economic systems, usually at the level of the nation state, have been predicated on the basis of doing everything possible to increase the wealth and prosperity of the country with little regard to the consequences elsewhere (particularly in the developing nations). Buddhist economics sees little problem with an economics that is beneficial to oneself, to one's business and to one's country, but only in circumstances of non-harm to others. In other words, establishing mutually beneficial transactions rather than exploitative ones is an important consideration of this type of approach. Indeed, the idea of mutually beneficial activities is a basic tenet that sustains Buddhist economics.

One distinguishing feature of Buddhism is that it has never engaged in a religious war. Its emphasis on peace and non-harm needs to be translated into modern economics. Non-harm means respecting all other humans and all other creatures, and developing a sense of the respect of all life. Such a stance is not only important at the level of the nation state, but also between businesses, at the community level and in exchanges between individuals. The approach here should also encompass tolerance, refraining from imposing judgements on the legitimate activities of others and promoting freedom. This is not to argue that people should simply be able to do anything that they wish, but so long as their activities are not causing harm to others there is no reason to impose any other set of values or rules on them.

An economics based on respect would certainly help to reverse the mounting ecological crisis which seems to be a characteristic of the 20th century. I have argued that economics should be based on notions of fair 'give and take', but this is missing when it comes to the environment, where we have developed a policy of 'take and take' without a thought to the consequences of such actions. Put simply, if we are going to take something from the environment we must be prepared to ensure that it can be replaced in one way or another. We need to develop a restorative economy where whatever damage is done to the environment is restored or fully compensated. We should remember that human beings are not the masters of the universe but a very small part of it. Thus it is the earth as a whole rather than human beings that must be placed at the centre of our worldview.

Buddhist economics is based on a common concept within Buddhism – the 'middle way'. Extreme views of the world are rejected since in such a diverse and changing time they can never encapsulate reality fully and by being extreme are unlikely to provide equal benefits to all creatures on the planet. Thus, both the extremes of a completely free market system and a completely centrally planned one can be rejected. Perhaps more importantly, however, the 'middle way' is also based on notions of moderation and it is this facet of Buddhist economics which makes it so powerful. If we were to emphasize moderation in all economic activities rather than optimization, this would have a radical and fundamental impact on the way we lead our lives and the way we treat the environment.

Moderation reflects the knowledge that Buddhists have that material possessions and consumption are not the root of happiness and contentment. The search for true happiness is not a material activity at all but a spiritual one. Reaching the goals of happiness and contentment requires us all, as individuals, to spend less time in consumption and more time in contemplation: less time following prescribed roles and more time being creative. Thus at the core of Buddhist economics is the need to recognize that as individuals we need to change and that once we do, institutions, businesses, governments and others will follow. We have a great window of opportunity to begin this peaceful individually-based revolution. The new millennium is a focus for change, with many people taking the milestone as an opportunity for change. Indeed, the time for change could not be better.

We should not underestimate the creativity of the human mind. It is one of the most important assets that we possess. It is creativity that has brought about some of the most beneficial changes we have seen in society and we need to harness that creativity to develop societies and economies that are more equitable, just and environmentally benign. However, creativity is best developed in a mind that is tranquil and not stressed. I always find it strange that businesses put so much pressure on managers who are constantly stressed, thus numbing their ability to develop creative solutions to business problems. If we could eliminate those levels of stress, we would create mindsets which are actually more flexible, leading to better business decisions, occasional brilliant insights and achieving the advances we need to see. Once again, though, developing the tranquil, creative mind requires us to abandon the psychological stress resulting from the mindset which demands people to do more and more in better and better ways. If our mindset was based more on moderation, then outcomes might be much more beneficial to all people and the planet.

Thus, as we can see, Buddhist economics is founded on changes at the individual level which will filter through to institutional change and begin to impact on the activities of governments and businesses. This is promising in some respects because rather than waiting for radical change through some sort of democratic process which is unlikely to happen, each of us can begin that change process now. In developing a spiritual attitude of caring and compassion we can improve our own lives, the lives of others and the planet as a whole.

BUDDHIST ECONOMICS IN BUSINESS

It should be made clear from the start that Buddhist economics is not anti-business or indeed anti-profit. It does stress, however, the importance of combining commerce with spiritual practice and sees business as being a considerable potential benefit and change if it is conducted along the lines of moderation. Moreover, it argues that the work of people is deeply worthwhile and itself is one path towards happiness and contentment. It calls on individuals engaged in work to reflect on their spiritual life in their activities and to be honest in their dealings. It advocates activities which benefit oneself only if they also benefit others, and stresses the need to care for all life and the environment. At all times business activities should be ethical, non-exploitative and non-harmful.

Business activities should be non-discriminatory and ensure that everyone involved in the business from employees to customers and suppliers are treated with the same respect. To do business according to Buddhist principles is to put oneself in a secondary place and put the emphasis on serving customers and everyone else involved in the process of exchange. It would be unacceptable to engage in any business activity where there was no thought of the consequences of the activity with regard to impacts on the world in which we live. Fundamental to the Buddhist approach is the idea that the activity itself should be an act of charity and service. That is not to suggest that we should expect people to work for nothing, only that the outcomes of any business activity should be fair and equitable.

Buddhist economics must reflect, of course, on the fundamental purpose for business activity. It must therefore have something to say about the role of profits. Fundamentally, however, the Buddhist motivation for work must be the pursuit of the interests of both oneself and others. The aim of making goods and providing services in a way which makes them affordable and accessible to people who need them is a just one. Therefore profit is not the principal goal of Buddhist economics, but neither are profits to be seen as something which is inconsistent with serving people and the planet. It is important to discuss how profits are made, because if they arise from the exploitation of people, animals or the environment, they would be seen as unacceptable. However, if they are the result of entrepreneurial activities that bring about a benefit to the world, they are to be celebrated. Buddhists would nevertheless have something to say about the distribution of profits, arguing that any share should be made on an equitable and just basis, and that profits should be in the interests of both oneself and others.

For Buddhists, any worldly activity should be directed towards learning and towards attaining happiness and contentment. Business has to be a part of this and has a role in providing both material and spiritual wealth. It is a fundamental part of what can help people to feel valued, worthwhile, secure and happy. It is a part of developing a balanced approach in our lives. Although Buddhists often stress the need for a minimum level of material wealth to sustain oneself, the ultimate goal is to secúre the happiness and contentment which we all desire. Traditionally, capitalism has tried to provide this happiness by providing more and more material objects. Buddhism, on the other hand, sees happiness not as a product of consuming more but as a product of desiring less.

Happiness might be seen as the ratio between wealth and desire (ie wealth divided by desire). The capitalist system has been quite successful in increasing levels of wealth and therefore increasing happiness to some extent. However, by increasing people's desires for more, stoking up avarice and greed, it has not produced great increases in happiness overall. The Buddhist approach would be for people to reduce their desires such that even the maintenance of current levels of wealth actually increase levels of happiness. In other words, as people become detached from desires, their happiness will increase. This may result, of course, in the reduced demand for many consumer goods. That should not be seen as a threat, but rather as an opportunity. It is an opportunity for businesses to concentrate less on providing non-essential consumer goods and to concentrate more on providing essential goods and services to developing countries, developing technologies which will remediate environmental damage and serving the poor and the needy. Indeed, business then naturally becomes less exploitative and damaging, and more worthwhile and productive.

The question then is what does a business look like in a world of Buddhist economics? In answering that question, the first thing to point towards is the recognition that our lives are dependent on other beings and that our lives are interconnected. Thus, the business is not a 'black box' of activities but rather a part of a network of complex and mutually beneficial arrangements. It is a business which recognizes the limits imposed on it by finite natural resources which need to be protected and is dependent on ensuring its continual survival by operating not only in its own interest but in the interests of all its stakeholders. It is a business which promotes Buddhist economic development and works for the benefit of all others, putting particular emphasis on helping those who are most in need. It is a business that promotes spiritual development within and outwith the organization.

The sort of spiritual community which a business can create is a much more open and eclectic one. The starting point is simply not to deny the link between the business community and the spiritual community. Work and the workplace are extremely important parts of the individual's spiritual development. It is difficult to embark on a spiritual journey without security in terms of an income. But it can be more than just a support mechanism for an individual's own journeys. The organization can actually begin to explore for itself. Cultural change, values redefinition and even traditional strategic planning can all involve searching for and exploring the new.

Recognizing and building on spiritual dimensions of work can begin to resolve this impasse. A Buddhist approach, for example, takes the function of work to be at least threefold: to give people a chance to utilize and develop skills and faculties; to help people to overcome their egocentredness by joining with other people in a common and fruitful task; and to provide the goods and services which are needed for oneself and others. This is hardly a radical departure from good employment practices, yet too often the emphasis is on the output and not on the human dimension of the workplace. Thus work is often organized in a manner which becomes repetitive, meaningless, boring and depressing. In effect it reduces the human to little more that the ubiquitous cog in an enormous machine, and work becomes soul-destroying.

Businesses can also be the focus for education. At heart, humans are contemplative and caring, but we have lost touch with that side of our personalities. This is often because we become little more than part of the overall system, and close relationships, trust, loyalty and love are all squeezed out. But it does not have to be like that – we simply need to learn and practise what comes naturally to us, given the space and energy. That process can happen within the family, within the workplace and anywhere else where we are in contact with each other.

The business and the people within it must realize the interconnectedness of all life. Too often we see the firm as having boundaries in terms of its locations and the products and services it provides and too often it shores up these boundaries as defensive strategies. Yet productive cooperation will always be superior to blind competition and recognizing cooperative opportunities is part of recognizing interconnectedness. The concept of interconnectedness also teaches us to value everything around us. When our production relies on raw materials from the developing world, for example, is it really acceptable to pay the lowest possible price for those raw materials, ensuring that people who work for us further down the supply chain are maintained in the present poverty of their lives? Is it right that our products should cause direct suffering on animals when we choose to test ingredients on them?

Although we have said that the business should not create boundaries that will remove it from the interconnectedness of nature, it is important for any organization to have a sense of place. Thinking globally and acting locally is not only a powerful strategy, it is a practical tool which can be used by the business to organize its environmental consciousness. Activities to promote local environmental improvement will be powerful if it is replicated elsewhere. Moves towards more regional models of industrial organization, local cooperation between businesses and the development of ecologically sensitive management systems can provide many advantages for both businesses and the environment.

Communion, compassion and humility have a very important role to play in the business organization. The spiritually aware, environmentally conscious firm is one where less emphasis is placed on top-down management and more emphasis is placed on cooperative, collective strategies. The egos of management are replaced by trust and all members of the organization are valued for their own skills and attributes. A caring work environment can actually enhance the performance of the business and make it a more humane place to work. The responsible and caring firm can also develop a passion for its own local environment, developing local nature conservation schemes, supporting local wildlife initiatives and being involved in local education programmes. These are practical strategies which the firm can undertake which nevertheless stem from recognizing a wider spiritual dimension to both the environment and the workplace.

The firm must also acknowledge its own change and impermanence and be prepared for changes that are inevitable. Holding on to fixed positions is simply bad business and the firm must be flexible and capable of change. But part of recognizing impermanence is also recognizing how transient material possessions are and how unimportant they can be compared with other spiritual aspects of the world. The firm does not exist in isolation, nor should it expect unstinting loyalty from its employees. Indeed, it should encourage a sense of non-attachment and encourage employees to have other interests. A programme of involving workers in community-based projects, helping them with their own further education and ensuring that there is not a culture in the organization which expects managers to work 70-hour weeks is a start.

Finally, any organization can be part of a reawakening process. It simply has to allow the people within it to explore new dimensions of spirituality. But the business must be awake itself to the changes that will occur as a result of a growing tide of spirituality. More will not be seen as better than less. There is likely to be more scrutiny with respect to the environmental and social impacts of products and processes. The company can choose to be a follower, but it is much more likely to be successful if it is a leader. To that extent the company should embark on its own reawakening and ethical and spiritual development through strategies that are associated with honesty, integrity, accountability and transparency.

BUDDHIST BUSINESS AND THE ENVIRONMENT

Traditionally, natural resources have been considered by businesses as available for their use to satisfy a set of desires which human beings have acquired. However, a Buddhist business would see the stock of natural resources as potentially available for use by all generations and therefore that stock has to be very carefully protected and used only when absolutely necessary. In particular, when we use natural resources we are borrowing from future generations and the cosmos and therefore they are not available for exploitation. Principles of non-harm and non-violence are therefore as equally applicable to the environment as they are to humans and other creatures.

We therefore need to persuade companies and the people within them not to use the environment either as an infinite source of potential profit or as a bottomless sink for waste. Business needs to make better long-term choices that assist in the preservation of our natural environment. Resources all serve a purpose; they are not simply inanimate and to destroy them is to have an impact on all interconnected things. When business realizes that we borrow natural resources from the environment and that their use will have a whole series of impacts, they will begin to make better choices and become stewards of the cosmos.

Many ecologists and philosophers in the past have noted that a society's level of civilization can be measured in terms of not only how it treats it citizens and how it respects all life, but also how it respects the environment upon which it so depends for life and continued existence. If we regard the environment as nothing more than a commodity, then sooner or later we will destroy the very thing that gives sustenance to life on our planet. As powerful actors in society, business has a significant role in realizing this and in explaining to others the consequences of continued environmental destruction.

As we have noted previously in this book, however, businesses can be great change agents and their potential to educate is considerable. Explaining the consequences of current economic systems that exploit the environment is only one facet of this education process. We have argued that the real solution lies in getting people to realize that being happy depends not on consumption and wealth but in freeing themselves from the desires that make them greedy. Business therefore has a role to play in educating its own workforce and its own consumers. It may seem odd in the present economic climate to call on businesses to convince their customers to buy less, but in reality that may be the only way to secure anything close to a sustainable future.

Buddhist businesses therefore have to establish new ways of thinking about the economy so that they can exist in an environment which is healthy and productive rather than in one which is sick and creates barriers to further development. We must move beyond using measures of profits and production as measures of success. In the past this type of approach has meant that the impact of production on natural resources, on the health of living creatures, methods of production and the human misery caused by both avarice and poverty have all become secondary issues. If we are truly serious about the existence of life on the planet, then we must ensure that all businesses carefully examine their impact on the environment, the physical and psychological health of their workers and the happiness of their consumers and suppliers.

THE END OF CONSUMERISM?

From a Buddhist perspective, consumption (particularly over-consumption and unnecessary consumption) is based on desire or greed. Buddhism shuns material desires because not meeting those desires (the norm) is the cause of great suffering. Buddhism can be viewed as a tradition that takes a moderate stance, however, and a certain degree of consumption is needed in order to sustain life. In other words, some basic desires are acceptable because they affirm that life. What Buddhism warns against is self-centred desire that in fact does not affirm life but eventually works against it.

Now we see a situation where the world's resources are in double jeopardy. Some commentators expect the world's population to double in the next 50 years and at the same time levels of consumption are rising, partly because of some alleviation of poverty but more so because of an increase in the desires of those who are relatively rich. It is clearly the problem of desire which needs to be addressed, since if the consumption levels of people living in the richest parts of the world fell, there would be enough ecological and economic space to accommodate rising populations. That is not to suggest that population control is unimportant, of course, but the main argument surrounds the need to distribute resources that can be produced in the world more equitably.

Of course, for many people the transition to a lifestyle of less rather than more will be a difficult one to make. People will have to come to realize what they suspect: that material possessions do not make people happy. Moreover, the Buddhist view of consumption reminds us clearly that happiness is not achieved by consuming more but by being able to be free from the chains of consumption and come to enjoy the simple, beautiful things in life, which are actually abundant and free.

The other side of the coin to not consuming more is, of course, wasting less. Indeed, we often measure production (at national and commercial level) in terms of output, but it would be applicable equally to examine production activities in terms of inputs and waste. More of an emphasis on producing and consuming the same amount of goods at lower input and waste levels would result in people leading just as happy a life. Indeed, if we also consume less, as Buddhists would propose, then the impact on the environment could be greatly reduced.

The consequence of the end of consumerism might be threatening to some, of course. There will be those who argue that reduced consumption will result in reduced production, and consequent unemployment and economic downturn. But this is a case of simplistic thinking in which one would be hanging on to lines of reasoning associated with traditional economics. It is true that people will be consuming less and there will be less produced, but this will also provide the opportunity for every person to work fewer hours and spend more time appreciating the simpler things in life. While people might work fewer hours individually, the total level of employment could easily remain the same. Moreover, if companies find themselves with spare capacity, they could concentrate their efforts on supplying goods to meet the needs of developing countries. Previously this may not have been so profitable, but with a reduced emphasis on the need to maximize profits and a new emphasis on doing business ethically and in the interests of others, such a strategy seems logical.

RIGHT LIVELIHOOD

As has been argued above, the work that an individual does is an important part of Buddhist practice. Having meaningful, rewarding and useful work is part of establishing an individual's 'right livelihood'. In contrast, too many people in the West (and elsewhere, indeed) view 'work as pain'. They work simply to provide the money for the consumption they desire. That does not create happiness – it simply becomes a source of suffering.

Of course, the profit motive has also tended to replace people with machines. Mechanization in many cases has meant that jobs have been lost and in other cases that work has become tedious, boring and unrewarding. That is not to argue that there should be some Luddite resistance, but it does suggest that we should think carefully about mechanization. We should distinguish between mechanization that improves and enhances human skills and the mechanization

145

that tends to make people slaves to machines. While we need to encourage better technology, this activity should not be at the expense of either becoming enslaved to machines or losing our ability to engage in honest hard work.

Every person in society can be both a consumer and a worker and Buddhists perceive this as involving a form of social service. Work is not only about making the means to sustain life but should also be about spiritual development. This means seeing work and the income it provides not only in terms of what it can do for the self but also in terms of what it can do for others. In particular, the work ethic should focus on human relationships, appreciating that work is done in the context of all kinds of human interactions that can be very rewarding. Whether as an employer or an employee, the Buddhist approach is to value their relationships.

In business we must realize that the company, its shareholders, employees, managers, customers and suppliers are all mutually dependent. People in the past will have made efforts to make the business successful. One of the aims of the business should be to ensure its survival into the future in order to provide benefits for future generations. This means that different people should be working together to achieve the same goals. Different people will have different roles and while it might be a manager's job to see to this, it does not mean that he or she has an inbuilt superiority over another human being. Indeed, one of the roles of management is to recognize the interconnectedness of all the relationships in a business and to try to manage these in the best interests of all involved. Respect, caring, understanding and doing the best for others are the values that should be at the heart of every exchange within the business.

CONCLUSIONS

Sustainable development is a radical concept and there is a need to take some quite radical moves if we are really to move to a situation which is environmentally responsible and socially coherent, and which satisfies the human spirit. What I have laid out in this chapter reflects the fact that technological fix, management systems solutions, culture change within the company, education and whatever else has been proposed within the current Western economic framework is, in fact, unlikely to be enough. Unless people change, unless we move away from a consumerist society and people regain a sense of spiritual well-being, I cannot see how we can sustain life on this planet despite the tools, systems and strategies we may come up with.

The challenge of the next 50 years must be to develop a human culture and an associated economic model which will save the earth rather than destroy it. A capitalist economy, Western aspirations, the process of globalization and an increasingly secular society will simply not produce anything close to sustainable development. Unless we are able to change people, we will end up changing very little.

In order to put into practice what I have advocated in this chapter, we must see economics and a moral and spiritual life as neither separate nor mutually exclusive. Buddhist economics is based on the premise that once we move away from compartmentalizing our lives to a new vision of what truly makes us happy and contented, then economics will follow and operate in a way that is spiritually rich, socially beneficial and environmentally friendly. While the 20th century has been marked by materialism, self-centred consumerism and greed, the 21st century needs to grasp spirituality, interconnectedness and moderation.

Buddhism is the way to attain much of what we need to achieve sustainable development. It provides an alternative to both the extremes of free market capitalism and state socialism. But it also adds something new: a quality which many people are searching for at the present time – it provides meaning to our lives. An emphasis on spiritual development, on simplicity and on caring for others is new and (for the West) radical. Buddhist economics is not threatening, as some in the West might see it. If properly thought through, it will lead to great change, but it will be change for the better as we are able to abandon the chains of consumption which bind us to suffering and realize our new potential to be different.

Chapter 7

Deep Change or Slow Death:
What Future for Business?[1]

THE NEED FOR CHANGE

The conclusion of this trilogy of books has to be that there is a need
for change in the way we do business. At the outset that change might
be associated with the introduction of management systems and tools
associated with improved environmental performance (the subject
matter of *Corporate Environmental Management 1*). However, as was
suggested in *Corporate Environmental Management 2*, such tools need
to be supported by organizational and cultural changes within the
organization if the process of continuous improvement towards zero
negative impact on the environment is to be achieved. In this book I
have gone one stage further in arguing that if businesses are serious
about the concept of sustainable development, then many of the
sacred tenets of doing business will have to be re-examined – the
business will have to think more clearly about ethics, about being a
campaigner and educator, and about making a closer link between
production and consumption, for example. I have suggested that one
way to achieve such a situation might be to examine closely more
spiritual dimensions of environmentalism and in particular Buddhist
approaches to economics and the environment.

---

1 The concepts of deep change and slow death come from one of the best books
on management which I have ever read: *Deep Change: Discovering the Leader
Within*, written by Robert E Quinn and published in 1996 by Jossey-Bass (San
Francisco). In a spirit of cooperation in achieving the changes we both see as
necessary, I have 'borrowed' these concepts and hope that they can convey to
readers of this book the same power that they have had on me.

Over the last ten years it has been interesting to see more and more businesses engage with environmental issues and introduce into their systems of operations a degree of care over the environment. More recently, the business world is beginning to engage with notions of social responsibility, but it finds that difficult because the issues are much more blurred and ill-defined. However, overall patterns of production and consumption have not really changed very much. Those of us in the West still consume many more times our share of the world's finite resources. Despite temporary economic setback, the trend in the East is towards better standards of living and increased wealth, created partly by a global shift of manufacturing industry to developing countries. With a doubling of the world's population expected over the next 50 years, it is therefore difficult to envisage the attainment of a situation which is consistent with sustainable development without even more significant change than even I have proposed in parts of these books.

My aim here in this concluding chapter is to go one stage further, therefore, in suggesting that there is a serious and urgent need for change in the way we do business, in the way governments and other institutions of power behave and in the way we as individuals lead our lives. I have come to believe, after ten years of working in the field of environmental management, that what is required is nothing less than deep personal change which will then permeate businesses and other institutions in an effective and radical way. We need also, of course, deep change in the way that business organizations are constructed but, in many ways, that will actually be a product of the change which will occur within the individuals who form part of that organization.

I do not underestimate that there is going to be a great resistance to deep personal and organizational change. For many individuals, confronting and experiencing a deep change in life is a frightening prospect, but those people who go through such change come out at the end feeling much happier and contented. I am sure that we all have friends who have changed careers at a time when their present one was safe and secure, who have downshifted their lives and who have rejected Western materialism in the search for something more simple and fulfilling. Their consistent message is that they have few regrets and wonder why they did not make the change sooner. Getting that message through to more people who often feel helpless and unable to move outside of the 'prison' of earning more money in order to spend more money will be difficult, I know. However, as we begin the new millennium, I believe that the potential for change and the speed of that change will accelerate. People expect something new and different to happen. Therefore, now is the time to begin to show individuals that deep personal change is both rewarding and, if we are serious about the planet on which we live and all its inhabitants, necessary.

We all have a role to play. Those of you who are reading this chapter with interest must realize that you have an obligation to become a leader in whatever capacity you can achieve. We all have the ability to become a leader who induces change. We are all potential change agents. We must begin our own process of personal change and when we have experienced the benefits of that change it will inspire us to help others to do the same. There is a need for everyone to open their minds to new possibilities. We need to respect ourselves more and to respect the life which surrounds us. By growing in our integrity, we can become part of a wider force for change which, I believe, is the only way to avoid chaos and catastrophe on the planet.

CHANGE IS ALL AROUND US

We live in a period of rapid change. Much of that change has been brought about through the rapid introduction of new technology, and future developments will revolutionize the way we communicate and socialize. There is a growth in the power of civil society in which various coalitions of people are demanding and achieving significant change. However, much of this change has brought about the distrust of many of the traditional institutions of power, including large business. Communications technology and particularly the Internet will make it easier for us to become part of a new drive towards the empowerment of people. At the moment, however, too many of us sit back and take on the role of the passive observer. In such a role we tend to become detached from what is happening around us and our sense of empowerment slowly decays. The fact that fewer and fewer people exercise their right to vote in democratic elections indicates that many people simply feel unable to be part of the change which is occurring around us and do not want to play an active role in shaping the future. In such circumstances people are experiencing a kind of slow death whereby their lives lack meaning and they simply become an insignificant cog in society's complex machinery.

Many of us often feel so powerless that we care not if we lose our integrity as human beings. Such a lack of integrity turns us into hypocrites: people who, for example, argue for increased care of the environment but do nothing personally about it. For me, therefore, the beginning of any change process within the individual involves increasing our sense of integrity and eliminating our hypocrisy gap. In doing that, individuals will change the institutions in which they work and with whom they engage. It does not require a majority of people to change in order to create change in an organization or in society as a whole. History has taught us that periods of beneficial change have often been created by a small group of people who have worked effectively together to create what they see as important. Of

150

course, there is a need for a critical mass of people to accept the direction of change, but we now live in a society where, perhaps more than ever before in history, people are yearning for that change to take place.

WHY DO WE NEED DEEP CHANGE?

It has been my assertion throughout these three books that if we are to take the environment and sustainable development seriously, there is a need for something more than marginal, superficial change. Marginal or incremental change is by definition somewhat limited in scope and it often becomes reversed over time. Putting a system in place to improve the environmental performance of business is a change in the right direction but it is not enough. Experience is already telling us that after a time such systems can break down when they are overtaken by more pressing concerns. And as I have argued previously, such marginal change can often lead to inertia, actually blocking any further change.

Deep change differs from marginal or incremental change in that it requires a much more systematic approach, involving new ways of thinking and behaving. But deep change is therefore highly risky and involves both individuals and organizations giving up 'security blankets'. Denial is commonplace: even among businesses that have been most proactive in the field of the environment, deeper change is terrifying and therefore rejected as being unnecessary. Only a small minority of business leaders have actively recognized the need for both deep personal change and a change in the way their business operates and behaves. I stress deliberately the need for both personal and organizational change because the two feed off each other. The lessons learned from one level of change can feed beneficial lessons into the other level. However, deep change at the organizational level requires first and foremost a change in the individual. Thus, for a business to change in a way which is consistent with sustainable development we have to see a significant number of people in that organization experiencing deep personal change in their lives.

Even when personal change does occur, that does not translate automatically into organizational change, however. Indeed, the concepts of organization and change are often in considerable conflict. The nature of an organization is one which is there to organize and that can therefore often be in conflict with any notion of change. The emphasis which businesses have put on quality systems and more recently on environmental management systems means that the activities of the business are often regularized, processes are documented and rigidly adhered to and products are standardized. While that can have benefits, it also means that we block change

151

because we create predictable behaviour rather than creativity. The great irony is that while the world around us is changing faster than ever before, organizations are increasingly systematizing everything they do, which makes them less able to respond to that change. Eventually, therefore, unless systems and organizations are constantly reviewed, re-evaluated and allowed to change, routine patterns of behaviour will move the organization towards decay and slow death. Although there are risks involved in stepping outside well-defined boundaries, we must do exactly that if we are going to create necessary change.

There is, therefore, a very close relationship between creating change within ourselves and change within the organizations with which we engage. To make deep personal change requires us to rethink our values, our skills, our needs and our desires. It involves re-evaluating everything we do and creating a new self that is more aligned to our inner beings and the world around us. There is therefore a need for us to take risks and confront our own hypocrisy. We need to learn to enjoy being different and to risk the unconventional. The path down which we travel cannot be mapped out in an exact way since the very change process which we experience will lead us to further insights and new developments. Essentially, the process of deep change involves stepping outside our comfort zones and our normal roles. In going through this process we come to realize that only by changing ourselves and by encouraging others to change as well can we bring about change in the world. By changing ourselves, learning from the experiences and becoming a leader and change agent, we really can have a positive impact.

Each of us has the potential to change. Many wish for change but feel helpless to begin the risky process. There is no doubting that the price of the change process can be high, but the benefits are also significant. Of course, it is easier to see the short-term risks than the long-term outcomes and therefore we are often blind to the possibilities which are there for us. There is, however, a price to pay for not engaging in deep change. The alternative is slow death.

THE SLOW DEATH OF THE ORGANIZATION

I have argued that many business organizations have real problems engaging with the rapid speed of change in the societies in which they operate. This means that they often make mistakes when they fail to recognize, for example, changing consumer demands, the power of pressure groups, public resistance to their activities and a great deal of scepticism from within and outwith the organization. Part of the problem in such circumstances, however, is not organizational at all but involves the inability of certain individuals to cope with their roles.

These people, the senior managers in an organization, are under daily pressures from a range of different stakeholders who produce more demands of them than they can possibly meet. Such people are tired and exhausted, become a function rather than a person, and do not have the space and the time to engage in the sort of creative thinking which can bring about much needed change in the organization. They are the leaders, but in many cases they fail to lead. Their stance becomes defensive, they reduce risks by keeping as much as possible under their own control, they have little vision, and they aggressively refute any external criticism.

Senior management is often completely ill equipped to deal with the realities of a changing world. The management tools which they use have been learned from other managers and in some cases from traditional business schools which still stress knowledge and functionality rather than skills and creativity. There is even inertia in the types of management styles being used in many organizations. So rather than create change within the organization, managers have a vested interest in maintaining the status quo where they are in more control of stable situations. In a rapidly changing world, however, such a stance can only lead to failure. And it is of little surprise that managers do not even think about the environmental and social consequences of their activities and act in a way which is totally at odds with the concept of sustainable development.

When you put pressure on people to achieve things which they cannot see a way of achieving, and at the same time it is accompanied by constant pressures to hit targets, achieve results, increase efficiency and take on more and more responsibility, people in any organization will be under more and more pressure. In order simply to appear to be coping, managers are forced to take short cuts and do not undertake tasks with the degree of care and precision that is really needed. In these circumstances a growing pressure is often put on people to engage in unethical behaviour. There is, in other words, a hidden power that encourages all sorts of corrupt practices and the exercise of power which is not in the interests of society as a whole.

Senior managers are therefore under great pressure, are drowning under the pressures enhanced by global competitive marketplaces and are often doing the jobs previously done by two or more people. Organizations expect managers to work harder and harder, which often translates into individuals working 70-hour weeks for a 40-hour salary. It is not surprising that many managers become self-interested, selfish and disinterested in the wider issues associated with sustainable development. Burnout is common and many managers find themselves experiencing periods of medication for stress. These people who should be undertaking a leadership position are often (literally) just fighting for survival and they do not have the energy, creativity or desire to initiate some sort of change process. In the intense battle of business, they become the walking wounded. They become the victims of the organizations they have created.

ORGANIZATIONAL CHANGE REQUIRES PERSONAL CHANGE

My assertion, therefore, is that if we are to create the sorts of changes in the business organization which can lead to change in the direction of sustainable development, we have to engage in deep personal change. Many of the systems and approaches we have in business are stagnant and are leading to the slow death of many of these organizations. These impediments to change have not appeared from nowhere, of course – they have been put in place by individuals. The same individuals can create deep change in an organization, which can revitalize its life in a way which is consistent with sustainable development. However, this requires deep change at the individual level. However, let me stress that it is not only those in managerial positions who need to change. For deep change to occur in societies which can shape the world in a way which is consistent with sustainable development, we all need to consider that deep change process. And whether we are consumers, producers, shareholders, managers or employees, we can all have an influence in creating a more sustainable business organization.

Many people, having been part of a change process in an organization, know that that process often fails. Once it has failed, any new change process is even more difficult to introduce since it is understandably treated with a high degree of scepticism. When a change process does fail, it is very common to blame others for the mistakes and take personal responsibility for the poor outcome. On many occasions change processes fail simply because the organization is expected to change in a way which is separate from the people within the organization. In other words, it is common to neglect the fact that if we want to bring about any change process, people involved in that change process have to change as well. Therefore, it is the inadequate preparation for change in terms of the individual him- or herself which can be a major barrier to success.

One key to successful change processes is strong leadership from empowered people who can shape and encourage others to change themselves. Empowered people have generally gone through change processes themselves, re-examining their values, beliefs and desires, and increasing both their integrity and credibility. Such people often engage in continuous personal change, spending time thinking and meditating, and taking the risks that are required for long-term personal fulfilment. Empowered people are very good at confronting themselves and challenging their own integrity. They are creative and open to new ideas and perspectives, but most importantly they are aware of their interconnectedness with the world, value diversity, and care about the damage and suffering which are often caused by the thoughtlessness of people with power.

For a process of change to bring about real environmental and social benefits, people need to be aligned with notions of ethics, equity and futurity. For us to achieve a situation which is consistent with sustainable development in a rapidly changing world requires us to recognize that, although we are tiny parts of the cosmos, nevertheless we can be change agents and bring about improvements in the lives of others in the world. We need, however, to be strong in ourselves if we are to be the initiators of beneficial change. That does not mean that we have to take a singular view and 'sell' it as hard as we can. On the contrary, it means recognizing our own continuous need for change and the need to both teach and learn. If we do not change, we cannot learn and we are less able to help others. If we allow ourselves to stagnate, we will begin to experience the psychological death which fuels a growing market for antidepressant drugs.

Therefore in embarking on our own personal journeys we need to leave aside our safe world of security. Such security, rather than making us happy, holds us back and creates the stagnation that we should avoid. We need to give up our traditional ways of thinking and to become open to new views and experiences. Indeed, we need to search out diversity and look for the messages which are all around us if we care to look for them. We need to engage actively with uncertainty and mysticism. As we begin to challenge and change some of our old paradigms, we will experience an expansion of our consciousness and begin to view the world differently. Care for the environment, a sense of interconnectedness, reducing our harmful actions and realizing that we are both (ironically) insignificant but also powerful, comes naturally. As we embark on such a process we will strive for even more personal change and that will naturally lead us to empower others. At that point we achieve the power to create change outside ourselves. But the inner change must come first.

As a starting point, individuals need to challenge their own perspectives on life and on the world around them. Of course, enlarging or changing our perspective is quite difficult to achieve because it means re-evaluating many of our actions in the past. Investments made in the past are not easy to put aside and it is difficult to reach the conclusion that we will have made a number of mistakes. Our present lives are very much a product of the past and it is therefore a formidable barrier to have to come to grips with tearing down and replacing some of our old assumptions and values. However, in order to progress and gain new insight, we must re-examine our beliefs and value systems.

One of the biggest problems that we have to overcome is our success. Whether it is success in gaining a university degree, in becoming a recognized expert or even becoming a chief executive of a large corporation, our apparent success is based, of course, on the decisions and effort we have made in our past. Therefore, the more successful we appear to be, the more difficult it is to challenge the past. Positive experiences and the feeling that we have done things well tend to make us believe that our worldview and our values and ambitions are correct. The more successful we are, the more we believe we are right and the more difficult it is therefore to change. Thus, in very powerful positions, whether it be in business or academia (in my experience full of professors with over-inflated egos) or somewhere else, we find an arrogant self-righteousness which is dangerous and stubborn. We must make sure, therefore, that our apparent success does not reinforce such a position. In making personal changes we will learn to challenge such single minded arrogance.

As we begin to reinvent ourselves, we all need to find a greater degree of humility in our lives if we really want to help others and recognize the wonder of nature, the importance of the environment and true care for others. We are all quite insignificant, but that should not be confused with being powerless. As we come to understand ourselves better, we will be able increasingly to connect with our current world. The process of deep change requires us to change our perspective, challenge our weaknesses, develop ourselves from within and redesign our paradigms. Perhaps more than anything, we need to develop our integrity and honesty. This means challenging our own fears, insecurities and hypocrisy. We must acknowledge our own greed, insensitivity and selfishness, and gain a clearer vision for the future. This is not an easy process and will lead to problems and difficulties. But not to do it will be worse.

Of course, the whole process of change has to be ongoing. It cannot be achieved overnight and we must hold on to the idea that change will take us in different directions at different times. This might lead to a sense of fear and insecurity, but it is also exciting and exhilarating. For the first time in my life, I have no idea whatsoever what I will be doing in five years' time. In the past it has all been mapped out and has been terribly predictable and boring. Now it is exciting and exhilarating to know that the future is a mystery. Recently, I decided to have an AIDS test. In waiting three days for the results I began to speculate about my future in the very unlikely event that it was positive. I considered the fact that I would probably have ten years of life for certain, given modern medical treatment, but after that nothing was certain. And I asked myself the question, 'What would you do now if you suddenly found that you had ten years to live?' The answer to that question was not difficult and involved a whole series of quite fundamental changes. But when the result eventually came back negative, I asked myself, 'So why are you not acting now as if you had only ten years to live?' The answer to that question was much more difficult, and raised many issues which I am still thinking about. I recommend it to you.

There is a Chinese proverb that I once learned from a wonderful man in Singapore. It goes along the lines of 'You do not have to steer the boat to get under the bridge'. The basic idea is that, as the boat gets nearer to a bridge, you do not have to steer it since it will simply be taken under the bridge by the natural currents. I translate this into meaning that you should not spend too much time planning ahead, but that you should take all experiences as meaningful and then progress as you learn, putting trust in what happens around you. It means that the direction of change will not be certain. It may well be that we have some sort of vision for the future, but it is far less likely that we will have a clear plan. We may know what the vision is, but we are less clear about how to get to it. That should not be seen as a problem, though. If the vision is strong and clear, you will move towards it. Do not worry too much about the details, just trust the vision, be flexible, be creative and listen. If we trust and believe in ourselves, we will get the signals to pursue the vision. Just go with the flow.

CHANGING THE ORGANIZATION

Defining an organization is difficult. An organization is often a group of other organizations and the organization that we have in mind might, with other organizations, be part of a bigger organization. One thing is certain, though; that is, the nature of organizations is constantly changing as a result of changes in the world around us. Successful organizations are able to adapt and be flexible. Others suffer from slow death. I argued strongly in *Corporate Environmental Management 2* that organizations have a culture and that culture will have a set of aims and objectives. Of course, those aims and objectives will be set by senior managers and therefore what usually happens is that the organization is there to serve the personal interests of top management. Traditional, rather naïve theories of the firm might tell us that it is ultimately shareholders who have the power, but experience tells us, of course, that as long as acceptable dividends are paid and share prices rise, managers are left to consume a good degree of profits within the organization.

Senior managers who want to make sure that their organization serves their needs therefore ensure that their aspirations are protected. Rules, regulations and structures are put in place to protect their positions and a change process is often difficult because it is impossible to penetrate the protective bureaucracy which has been created. The whole organization becomes wrapped up in a strong corporate culture and it is difficult to achieve anything that is perceived as deviant. In such circumstances managers often pay lip service to environmental issues, but to undertake the deep changes demanded by the concept of sustainable development is seen simply as a bridge too far, which would upset the status quo.

When organizations do undergo deep changes it is often brought about by external pressures: loss of market share, falling sales, customer complaints, adverse publicity or adverse campaigns by pressure groups, for example. In such circumstances the organization is forced to behave in a reactive, unplanned sort of way. More than any other strategy, however, the usual approach will be to fix the problem without upsetting too many of the structures already in place to protect the corporate élite. In such circumstances the dominant figures in the organization are clearly not interested in deep change. There is no real vision.

What we find, therefore, in most organizations is that although incremental and marginal change is possible sporadically, the dominant culture in the organization is often untouchable. As a result, the organization breeds inertia, rigid structures and a good degree of dispondency on the part of the people who are affected. Many people find themselves having to engage in tasks which they see as unimportant simply because 'that is the way we do things around here'. This creates a downward cycle of pessimism and a lack of any sense of meaning. It is no wonder that so many people go into minor depression on a Sunday evening when the prospect for the following day is work.

But the real problem is not an external one. It is not even a problem associated with a corporate culture based on the vested interests of a few. The real problem is within each of us, and deep change in any organization must begin with personal change. It is all too easy simply to blame the external pressures or the corporate culture. Each of us can be a source of change by changing ourselves and building coalitions of like-minded people. Of course, senior management ethics can be pervasive, but these are simply other human beings who, deep down, are searching for their own personal change as well.

Without deep personal change I would argue that organizations simply cannot change. It might be possible to tear down the old systems and hierarchies which make the organization such an unpleasant place, but unless people within the organization also change at a personal level, new equally destructive systems and hierarchies will re-emerge. It is only when we discover new values and new paradigms that change can be long lasting. But organizational change also requires creative, systematic thinking. It means looking beyond the scope of any immediate problems and finding the actual source of the trouble. Businesses that pay mere lip service to environmental protection, for example, must come to realize that the death of the environment actually results in the death of business. Moreover, business has to realize that if we do not internalize concepts which are associated with sustainable development, the future of everything which currently holds society together is under threat.

What this implies for business is quite clear. As I have argued in these three books, there is a need for a change in paradigms. Indeed, a movement through a number of paradigms is required, and as the personal change I have spoken of develops, so it will be easier to progress along these paradigms. These paradigms should not be seen as mutually exclusive but ones which build on each other. They are summarized in Table 7.1. Once the business organization has accepted the need to tackle its environmental problems, it can progress along what I call a technical paradigm (which is largely dealt with in *Corporate Environmental Management 1*).

The technical paradigm is based on the use of systems and associated tools. The source of the power is based on a degree of technical competence, with the credibility of the organization enhanced by the use of standards. The environmental ethic is clearly one of emphasizing improved environmental performance. The corporate culture is really no different from that which is found in any organization having a traditional hierarchical, divisional structure, and therefore could be considered as tactical and confrontational. This is so often the case in businesses which create environmental management teams outside other functions, resulting in conflict between those who want to raise the profile of environmental issues and others with completely different (more traditional) business objectives. Behaviour patterns within the organization tend therefore to be individualist, with the overall objective being personal survival. The biggest potential problem in the field of corporate environmental management is that companies adopt this paradigm and do no more. One can see easily that without any matching individual change, the environmental efforts the company makes could always be threatened and lost when other priorities arise.

In *Corporate Environmental Management 2* we argued therefore that real environmental success would only be achieved within the organization if there was a greater emphasis on what we might now call the culture change paradigm. Here the nature of the system is based on organizational learning, meaning that the company is better able to adapt on a long-term basis to changing environmental demands. The source of power lies in effective transactions that seek the attainment of shared values and visions in the organization. The

Table 7.1 *Paradigm Development for Corporate Environmental Management*

	Technical paradigm	**Culture change paradigm**	**Transformational paradigm**
Relevant book in the trilogy	Corporate Environmental Management 1	Corporate Environmental Management 2	Corporate Environmental Management 3
Nature of the organization	Systems based	Organizational learning	Moral system
Source of power	Technical competence	Effective transactions	Core values
Source of credibility	Standards	System of exchange	Personal integrity
Environmental ethic	Improved environmental performance	Respect for nature and people	Sustainable development
Corporate culture	Tactical and confrontational	Rational and conceptual	Self-authorizing
Behavioural patterns	Individualist	Cooperative	Diverse and unconventional
Overall objective	Personal survival performance to targets	Success of the organization	Visions attainment

Source: adapted from Quinn, 1996

source of credibility comes from a common knowledge that the organization is a system of exchange where the effective transactions lead to superior outcomes. The environmental ethic revolves around a respect for nature and a respect for people. The corporate culture is rational and conceptual, with people moving beyond traditional divisional tensions and an attempt to see environmental improvement as a collaborative effort. Behaviour patterns are therefore cooperative. The overall objective is the success of the organization.

In this book, I have tried to extend the analysis of corporate environmental management in dealing with the challenges associated with sustainable development. Essentially, this means switching to a third paradigm which I have called the transformational paradigm. Here the emphasis is on transforming the organization into one which is working in a way which is consistent with sustainable development and all the various elements of that concept. The nature of the organization becomes based on shared values and beliefs based on a moral system. The organization extends it natural boundaries, seeing itself not only as a business but also as an educator and campaigner with this in mind. The source of power comes from core values which are commonly held in the organization and the source of credibility is a result of the personal integrity of those involved within the organization. Clearly, the environmental ethic is extended to encompass sustainable development. The corporate culture is self-authorizing, where great emphasis is placed on individuals changing with the organization and taking more responsibility for their own actions. Behaviour patterns therefore tend to be diverse and unconventional. The overall objective of the organization is to attain its vision, which will include acting in a way which is consistent with sustainable development.

The transformational paradigm is fundamentally different from the first two paradigms because of its emphasis on personal change. Indeed, this paradigm is achievable only if people have gone through a process of change whereby they are able to be much more self-authorizing and place a great emphasis on personal integrity. Such a process of change is needed so that members of the organization can see things clearly, appreciate diversity and become part of a common vision based on shared values and beliefs which have been developed within the organization. Of course, moving to such a paradigm requires great leadership from within the organization and this is perhaps why few firms will ever achieve such a position in the short run. However, over time, as the importance of sustainable development is more appreciated or the consequences of not moving in that direction begin to be realized, there is likely to be more progress made. Until then, I would put my own emphasis on each one of us experiencing our own deep change processes.

CREATING CHANGE AND BUILDING CREATIVITY

I have argued earlier in this book that traditional systems approaches tend to create a degree of inertia. Inevitably, this will be in conflict with the need for organizations to be more and more flexible in a world which is more and more uncertain and dynamic. There will be a need for organizations to change more rapidly in the future than they have ever done in the past. Moreover, if companies are going to take advantage of new opportunities in the future, they will also have to be creative in finding new modes of production and distribution, new forms of organization, new partnerships and an increased responsiveness to the demands of stakeholders. To put it simply, they will have to be creative in finding new ways of doing business which are consistent with changing times and the need for a commitment towards sustainable development.

Effective organizations in the future will need to embrace change and uncertainty. In order to do so they will have to demonstrate four key characteristics: agility, integration, participation and the ability to think differently.

Agility

The future will be characterized increasingly by fast and unpredictable change. Organizations therefore need to be responsive and not tied down to inflexible systems. The complexity of modern society means that it is difficult to make 'safe' forecasts and there may be periods of turbulence where the organization has to adjust in quite radical ways. Companies need to be able to respond quickly, therefore, and to have the flexibility to react in creative ways.

Traditional systems cannot deliver this sort of agility. They tend to tie down the organization and its various functional divisions to certain modes of activity and actually restrict the freedom the organization has to develop new ways of doing business. This can reduce the opportunities which are available to the company and restrict its ability to respond to changing market circumstances and changing demands from stakeholders. Systems standards such as ISO14001 can lock a company into certain environmental protection measures without sufficient reference to the wider implications for sustainable development, for example.

Integration

There is a need to see the company as a total system because in that way the organization is better able to respond to change and take advantage of new opportunities. There should be less dependence on functions which can give the organization too narrow a focus. A whole range of functions which are available in the organization need to be considered as a whole and combined to find solutions.

There is a need to move beyond traditional systems and systems thinking towards more systematic thinking which is able to deliver new solutions for new problems. Only by taking a broad systematic view of the organization and its interactions can we ever hope to recognize fully a way in which to engage with the demands of moving towards doing business so that it is consistent with sustainable development.

Participation

Everyone in an organization has the potential to create change which is good for the company. However, they need to be allowed freedom and to be empowered to take more responsibility for their own functions. Management has a role in creating an atmosphere where innovation and creativity are rewarded. There need to be adequate incentives for employees to break out of the routine, ritualized mode and develop more flexible and responsive modes of work.

Participation has a long history in business research. Survey after survey has shown the benefits of working in more participative environments, yet so many companies hold on to rigid hierarchical management systems which tend to stifle the benefits of working in a participative way. But it is not only good business to encourage participation and involvement in the organization, it is also more consistent with a move towards sustainable development whereby people must not only participate in a change process but must also take on more responsibility for the planet in every aspect of their lives.

The ability to think differently

It has been argued before that systems can often lead to inertia, and in order to avoid this companies need to encourage innovative and creative behaviour. Each process needs to be examined and those responsible for each process encouraged to come up with suggestions to make it more effective. New demands placed on the company need to be met with new products, new processes and developing rather than rigid systems. Indeed, it will be most effective if the company considers new organizational forms in order to stimulate creativity and break down artificial functional barriers.

Thinking differently means that the company must move away from simple solutions to an environmental crisis and growing social inequity. It will not be enough simply for businesses to adhere to environmental management systems standards if our ultimate aim is to move to a situation which is consistent with sustainable development. There is a need to think about new ways of doing business, new priorities for production and consumption, and new ways of behaviour towards each other. Businesses can and must take a lead, but that will require them to put aside traditional modes of operation and begin to think differently.

BARRIERS TO CHANGE

The process of deep change is not an easy one. The organization itself is likely to be a complex one, such that no two people will describe it in exactly the same way. Indeed, no individual is likely to be able to describe the whole system. We cannot avoid people having different perspectives on how the organization functions and operates, but we can aim at a degree of convergence and agreement relating to core values and the basic principles of operation. Put simply, different parts of an organization will tend to see things differently. Individuals like to hold on to their own perceptions of reality rather than see the picture as a whole. This can paralyse the organization in a period when change is needed.

Systems in the organization are very complex, of course, and increasingly dynamic. The temptation to simplify systems and flow chart operations is therefore understandable, but this does tend to stifle the very dynamic in the organization which can produce flexibility and creative behaviour. It is tempting to break down the organization into parts or functions so that it can be managed and monitored more easily, but the more efficient way of working in an uncertain future is to integrate those parts together. The natural unwillingness to deviate from current modes of practice needs to be broken down and people should be encouraged to step outside over-rigid systems. There is a need to switch from conservative modes of behaviour towards one where taking risks is allowed and where making mistakes is acceptable.

Unlearning is often the first step to change. Just because an organization has been successful in the past does not guarantee it a future. Yet that very success makes people feel smug and secure, and that can lead to complacency. If people are arrogantly confident about how well they are doing, that will lead to inertia and an inability to recognize the need for doing things differently and even better. In order to stay dynamic, there is a need to re-evaluate constantly what is going on and to recognize change as somewhat inevitable. Therefore, people often need to unlearn the old ways of working and ingrained habits. They need to recognize new opportunities. Here, communication is important and a key role for management is to question and challenge current work practices constantly.

Often there is a reluctance on the part of people to accept the need to change unless a feasible solution is in sight. Again, that tends to lead to the inertia which can weaken the organization. Middle management in particular will resist change because they will see it as a threat to themselves. They will tend therefore to be averse to risk and to put barriers in the way of the change process. They will engage in political infighting rather than work together to find creative solutions.

PROVIDING THE CONDITIONS FOR CREATIVE BEHAVIOUR

The first thing to recognize in any organization is that there is a need to change. We know that without change in the way we produce, distribute and consume goods there will be a growing threat of environmental catastrophe. Without change, organizations will not survive in a fiercely competitive international economy. Therefore, within any organization there needs to be a dialogue on the nature and direction of change. The organization and the people within it need to ask where the company is, why it has been successful in the past, how it can be successful in the future and in which direction it is to progress. This needs to be an open dialogue and one where every person is encouraged to make a contribution.

In most organizations it is unacceptable and seen as a failure when people make mistakes. This tends to stifle creativity because people are unwilling to experiment with new ideas in case the outcome is unsuccessful. Therefore, people should be given opportunities to experiment and not be criticized for making mistakes if they occur. This means breaking down vested interests and eliminating the functional infighting which so often exists. It means celebrating effort rather than outcomes. Only by allowing experimentation will creativity be achieved.

Change also needs to become a collective process. People should not sit back and watch but should become involved in the change process. This means creating shared perceptions based on common values and visions. Management, and particularly senior management, need to be clear about those values and encourage everybody to work towards them. But they also need to create a climate of openness and debate within the organization so that people can challenge some perceptions in a way which leads to productive debate rather than ridicule.

Analysis and diagnosis

In order to put a change process in place and encourage creativity there needs to be a process of analysis, followed by the identification of barriers to change in order to overcome obstacles. This is not a one-off effort but part of a process, of continuous improvement. This can be an effective diagnostic process but it needs to be managed carefully to avoid the political infighting which so commonly exists within organizations. This means shifting away from blaming individual people and departments and analysing the whole system. It means seeing a problem as everybody's problem. So in our example, rather than blame the design department for poor documentation, the sales and planning function needs to help to solve the problem by telling the designers just what type of documentation would be of most use to them.

Education and training

It has already been argued that effective communications are a vital part of any change process which aims to bring about creativity. This needs to be supplemented with effective education and training so that everybody understands the message and is committed to finding new ways of doing things. Involving different functions in the same training events is one way to start breaking down interdepartmental rivalry and create an awareness of the need to work more closely together. Effective training and education can build up eagerness and momentum and is therefore a vital part of any change process.

Educational seminars where new solutions are discussed, where systems are reconsidered and where there is an element of planning involved in the event can be very successful. Indeed, the process of change can become one of excitement if everyone is involved in it. However, if that involvement and participation is missing, it can easily become a process of fear and alienation where people do everything in their power to stop the change and protect their own interests at the expense of others.

People increasingly need to be trained in handling complexity. Indeed, much of the education which exists in schools, colleges and universities ignores this. Yet in the future, handling uncertainty, complexity and change will be a vital management function. New skills need to be developed which will enable managers to manage diversity, turn conflict into opportunity, and stimulate experimentation and creativity. The problem with the traditional systems-based approaches is that commonly they stifle such things.

Generating creativity

Traditional systems tend to stifle creativity. They tend to rely on there being rigid structures in place which can encourage the functional battles which are so damaging to an organization. At the core of any change process is the need for creativity, and there needs to be a process of encouraging and developing that creativity in the organization. This means seeing the organization in a larger context, being willing to take risks and becoming increasingly participative in all operations. Space needs to be made for encouraging creativity.

Systems, of course, are not unimportant, but we must move away from those systems which create inertia towards systems which encourage systematic thinking and creativity. Trying out new ideas needs to become legitimized and the creative process needs to be rewarded. Failure should not been seen as something to be admonished but as a process from which there should be lessons learned. There are constraints to creativity, but many of them exist only in the minds of people who feel frightened or threatened by change. This needs to be overcome through a policy of involvement and dialogue. Dreams have to be allowed and encouraged.

Participation

The leaders of an organization can only lead if they have committed followers. Commitment comes from trust, a shared belonging, and common values and visions. The most effective leaders are therefore likely to be those who can bring people along with them in a participative way, valuing the contributions which everyone can make to the organization, and engaging in open and honest dialogue. However, increased participation is not a one-way street. Along with participation comes responsibility, and the full benefits of participation will only be achieved if those participating become more responsible for their actions and more committed to achieving the visions of the organization.

The development of trust between all members of an organization is one of the biggest challenges to achieve. Breaking down a history of distrust and conflict is often not easy, but is vital if the organization is to move forward in an effective way. One of the major functions of management is to build that trust, work together and demonstrate the benefits of holistic thinking rather than departmental rivalry.

Values and visions

All organizations have values. Many organizations are not aware of those values until they start to think about their behaviour – and then they are quite surprised. Organizations which turn a blind eye to unethical practices are effectively condoning them. Those that harm the environment needlessly clearly have no regard for future generations. Those with only men in senior management positions are displaying a degree of sexism which they often deny if they are confronted directly with such an allegation. The only way, therefore, for the organization to ensure that it has the values with which it wishes to be associated is for it to be transparent and open about them.

Based on the values which the organization has, it can then produce visions of what it would like to become in the future. These visions are effectively a form of normative forecasting. They might be considered dreams for the future based on a number of different scenarios and perspectives. They will include visions of how the organization would like to treat its employees, customers and other stakeholders. They should also demonstrate the value attached to environmental improvement through visions of being an environmentally benign company or one which campaigns for sustainable development.

In order to create visions it is important to have pictures of the future. A vision of what a factory will look like in 5 or 10 or 20 years will tend to stimulate people to work in that direction if those visions are commonly aspired to. The process of vision creating should be a participatory one, therefore, whereby everyone can see the benefits of working towards common goals and aspirations. Visions of a better working environment, of a clean and healthy workplace, and socially and environmentally responsible modes of doing business will be embraced by people who see the benefits for themselves and others. Visions cannot be imposed, therefore – they need to be negotiated and discussed so that there is a common commitment to creating the change which is needed to achieve the end result.

Visions require blueprints and plans of action. The organization and everyone within it needs to be able to see the path towards the future. That path may not always be an easy one and visions may have to be amended from time to time. Visions should not be single-minded, however. It is important to bring together alternative ideas and develop a holistic outcome which is capable of achieving different people's aspirations. In other words, a vision must offer something for everybody in the organization. At times the journey towards the vision of the future will require experimentation and risk taking, and that process will be much easier if everybody is working together to the same ends. Simple systems will not be enough; a vision for the future requires exploration and creativity if it is to be achieved.

CREATING THE VISION

Without a clear vision a company will not have a clear idea about which path to travel down and will find strategic planning a pointless exercise. But a vision is more than just a map of where to travel: it gives a company its identity and should be a product of the coming together of the company's core values. In many ways a vision of where the company wants to be in the future and of what it stands for gives the company meaning and life. Without such a vision a company is just a mechanistic framework for making money, often in a sporadic and reactive way. As I have argued throughout this final chapter, however, it is not the company alone that needs to have a vision, but also those who work within it. Managers in particular need to find their own visions of the future.

Having a clear vision helps both the company and its managers to overcome much of the short-term thinking which is so common in business organizations. The bureaucratic structures which I have discussed above, along with internal (often personal) conflicts, political manoeuvring and the emphasis on the status quo, are symptoms of a company without a clear vision of what it is and what it wants to become. But a vision is more than just a mission statement which often lays out, in bland and often unbelievable principles, what the company's objectives are. Real vision comes from the soul of the company and the people within it, and represents a statement of belief. In many ways it presents a dream which is worthwhile striving for. For many companies their vision will represent a new world view which is consistent with the principles of sustainable development. And we must recognize that without that vision on the part of business, moving towards situations which are consistent with sustainable development is going to be very hard to achieve.

As with the organizational change discussed above, it is important to recognize that developing a vision for an organization has to begin with the people within that organization. They need to have their own visions of the future and they need to be allowed to develop and discuss those visions with others. Thus a process of empowerment is vital if people are to be given enough confidence and space to explore their values and visions, and to engage with others in meaningful discussion and debate. There also needs to be an atmosphere of creativity and experimentation whereby mistakes are learned from rather than (as is often the case) punished. Perhaps the most important thing which senior managers can do is to provide the inspiration for people to think about issues that will affect them and the organization in the future. High on the list of priorities here must be the environment and sustainable development.

The whole process of vision development requires strong leadership from the top of the organization, which should be cascaded down to middle managers who will be vital in the process of empowering all people in the organization. It is interesting that people who have significant responsibilities for the operation of part of a company are called managers. To manage means to organize, to control, to direct and to cope with. Management, therefore, can end up being little more than another process in the organization. What would be the effect if we were to change our usual terminology and call such people leaders? To lead means to inspire, to guide, to go in front and to show the way. What a different role that is! While the process of management is obviously important, good quality leadership is needed if the company is to develop and achieve its vision for the future.

Throughout these three books there has been a constant reminder that to move towards sustainable development requires change. In this book it has been argued that that change needs to be fundamental and deep. Equally, we need to build creativity in the organization, where experimentation is allowed and where people are empowered to express their own visions and contribute to the overall purpose of the organization. In Figure 7.1 there are two axes. On one we have a spectrum which begins with no change and ends with deep change. On the other, we have an axis which is the spectrum between creativity and stability. This clearly gives us four quadrants.

Figure 7.1 *Organizational Types*

In the top left-hand quadrant, we have the stifled organization where, although there is a degree of creativity, it can never be fully realized because the company will only allow creativity within the overall constraints of the status quo. The status quo might allow a degree of new product development and technological innovation, but that development will be bound by the need to adhere to certain set structures, objectives and a rigid corporate culture. In an organization which allows a degree of creativity but is unwilling to go through a change process, we find that the creative element soon burns itself out. This leads to frustration, to internal conflicts and eventually to a situation where people will simply come to work to earn their money and then go home again.

In the bottom left-hand quadrant we have the frigid organization which lacks life, dynamism and is passionless. It is essentially a mechanistic organization, which emphasizes management systems, order and control. Creativity rarely exists because there are few incentives to experiment with. Mistakes are punished and managers are rewarded by attaining fixed targets. This is the type of organization in which there is a great deal of inertia, where there are many managers and no leaders, and where a 'business-as-usual' mentality allows no room for the widening of any of the aims and objectives of the business.

In the bottom right-hand quadrant we find the realm of the stalled organization. It is likely that here we will find many individuals who are going through a personal change process and are encouraging the organization to do the same. However, the emphasis on stability means that the company is unwilling to allow the space for creativity and change to develop in the organization as a whole. This is the type of company where people are moving on in their lives and begin to see that their future is not within a company which cannot cope with the same sort of change process. The organization therefore sees many of its best managers and workers leaving to find places of work which are much more fulfilling and more consistent with their own change processes. The organization needs to take risks if it is to benefit from the change process but is unable to do so, usually because it lacks leadership at the top.

In the top right-hand quadrant we have the visionary organization. Here there is an alignment between personal and organizational change. It is a situation where creativity, empowerment and leadership throughout the organization are encouraged and rewarded. Here the organization is able to develop its values and visions, and the direction of the company then becomes clear, ambitious and exciting for everybody involved. There is a clear sense of purpose in the organization. It is only in this quadrant that we will find organizations which are able to appreciate and operationalize the changes which will bring about situations consistent with sustainable development.

Therefore it is clear that we need to develop organizations and the people within them which are both more creative and able to recognize the importance of change. People within such an organization become self-authorizing, often follow unconventional methods and their actions are based on moral principles rather than business-as-usual. This is the type of organization where deep change is possible, and indeed the only type of organization which, in a tumultuous world, can avoid slow decay and death.

THE PROCESS OF CHANGE

The challenge for the modern business organization which is serious about the concepts inherent in the idea of sustainable development is to move towards becoming a visionary organization. It involves the transformation of the organization. Again, I would put the initial emphasis on the people in the organization, who must begin to work as a trusting team rather than (what is more common) a coalition of different people with different interests whose basic aim is personal survival. Of course, some individuals will make personal sacrifices for the good of the organization, but they will only be willing to do that for a company which has built up a set of shared values and visions.

Transformation involves people abandoning their own self-interest, distrust, egotism and political posturing. The distrustful climate which is so common in many organizations needs to be replaced by one of cooperation, where people are working towards goals which they recognize are better for themselves and better for the organization as a whole. Strong leadership will be needed to achieve this situation and people need to experience the process of empowerment that allows them to be creative and to experiment. But experimentation also requires careful evaluation and reflection if the lessons of risk taking are to be truly worthwhile. There are no simple checklists which are capable of mapping out the path of change. It will be different for each individual and each organization. However, I have laid out in this chapter some important principles. Perhaps most importantly, though, individuals and organizations need new paradigms – ones which are consistent with sustainable development.

Such new paradigms involve embracing uncertainty in a rapidly changing world and realizing that unless there is deep change, there may not be any significant future to talk about. Current languages associated with business emphasize the status quo. To organize often means to systematize, to order and to control. It is no wonder, therefore, that businesses find it so difficult to engage with social and environmental issues when they have problems seeing outside the narrow mindsets imposed by notions of growth, market share, profit maximization and shareholder value. The new organization will have to be much more flexible and adaptive, exploring risk and generating high levels of creativity.

When we study ecology we know that, in order to survive and remain healthy, any vibrant species needs to adapt and transform. All systems must expand and grow, otherwise they decay into a state of slow death. Organizations are no different. More than anything, though, I have come to believe that individuals and organizations have to go through a process of deep radical change if we are to reverse the huge damage caused to our planet in the last century. The process of deep change requires us all to think again about the fundamental values in our lives. It requires us to regain our connectedness with nature and our sense of spirituality. This has to be discussed in places where it is often not discussable: in the organizations in which we work.

Our starting point has to be our own integrity. Most of us have an incongruity between whatever values we possess and our actual behaviour. There is a need to create a strong vision for the future and our role within that. Of course, this is not an easy process and for many it can be quite painful. It requires much more than superficial analysis: it requires deep meaningful thought and meditation if we are really going to discover our true selves. But if we are going to create a difference, the change process needs to be discussed. Going through some sort of individual transformational process needs to become a valid and interesting point of discussion and not something we feel embarrassed to admit. The minority of people who are currently engaged in such a process need to work together to form a critical mass. Then we may begin to see real change in our organizations and in our societies. Only in those circumstances will we see real progress towards sustainable development.

MAKING A DIFFERENCE

What is the point of life if we cannot make a difference? It is not enough for us just to exist; our aim in life is to make a contribution and to make the world a better place for all its inhabitants. But making a difference is important for both the individual and the organization. And the organization, because it has more power and influence than most individuals, is capable of bringing about even greater changes and making even more of a difference. If we are serious about sustainable development, we will have to make things different. The truth that we must accept is that sustainable development is about change and requires change. Unless we are willing to go through a process of deep change, all we will see is slow death.

References

CHAPTER 1

Brown, L (1991) 'The new world order', in L Brown et al, *State of the World 1991*, Earthscan, London

Carley, M and Christie, I (1992) *Managing Sustainable Development*, Earthscan, London

Carson, R (1965) *Silent Spring*, Penguin, Harmondsworth

Daly, H E (1996) *Beyond Growth: The Economics of Sustainable Development*, Beacon, Boston, Mass

Derrida, J (1978) *Writing and Difference*, Routledge and Kegan Paul, London

Durning, A (1991) 'Asking how much is enough', in L Brown et al, *State of the World 1991*, Earthscan, London

Elkington, J and Burke, T (1987) *The Green Capitalists*, Gollancz, London

Engel, J R and Engel, J G (1990) 'The Ethics of Sustainable Development', in J R Engel and J G Engel, *Ethics of Environment and Development: Global Challenge, International Response*, Belhaven, London

Gergen, K (1992) 'Organization Theory in the Postmodern Era', in M Reed, and M Hughes, *Rethinking Organization*, Sage, London

Gladwin, T N, (1993) 'The Meaning of Greening: A Plea for Organizational Theory', in K Fischer, and J Schott (eds), *Environmental Strategies for Industry*, Island Press, Washington DC

Hall, S and Jacques, M (eds) (1989) *New Times: The Changing Face of Politics in the 1990s*, Lawrence and Wishart, London

Harvey, J (1989) *The Condition of Postmodernity*, Blackwell, Oxford

Hassard, J and Parker, M (eds) (1993) *Postmodernism and Organizations*, Sage, London

Hirsch, F (1977) *Social Limits to Growth*, Routledge and Kegan Paul, London

Pepper, D (1993) *Eco-socialism: from Deep Ecology to Social Justice*, Routledge, London

Piore, M and Sabel, C (1984) *The Second Industrial Divide*, Basic Books, New York

Power, M (1990) 'Modernism, Postmodernism and Organizations', in J Hassard and D Pym (eds), *The Theory and Philosophy of Organizations*, Routledge, London

Schumacher, E F (1974) *Small is Beautiful*, Abacus, London

Steward, F (1989) 'Green Times', in S Hall and M Jacques (eds), *New Times: The Changing Face of Politics in the 1990s*, Lawrence and Wishart, London

Tokars, B (1987) *The Green Alternative*, R and E Miles, San Pedro, California

Welford, R J (1997) *Hijacking Environmentalism: Corporate Responses to Sustainable Development*, Earthscan, London

Welford, R J and Gouldson, A P (1993) *Environmental Management and Business Strategy*, Pitman Publishing, London

UNDP (1992) 'Human Development Report 1992', Oxford University Press, Oxford

World Commission on Environment and Development (1987) 'Our Common Future', Oxford University Press, Oxford

CHAPTER 2

Argyris, C (1964) *Integrating the Individual and the Organization*, John Wiley, New York

Bennis, W (1972) 'A funny thing happened on the way to the future', in J Thomas and W Bennis (eds), *The Management of Change and Conflict*, Penguin Books, Harmondsworth

Burke, T, Maddock, S and Rose, A (1993) 'How Ethical is British Business?', Research Working Paper, Series 2, Number 1, University of Westminster

Burns, T and Stalker, G (1963) *The Management of Innovation*, Tavistock Press, London

DiMaggio, P J and Powell, W (1983) 'The Iron Cage Revisited: Institutional Isomorphism and Collective Rational in Organizational Fields', *American Sociological Review*, 48, 147–60

Donaldson, J (1989) *Key Issues in Business Ethics*, Academic Press Inc, San Diego

Donaldson, J and Waller, M (1980) 'Ethics and Organization', *Journal of Management Studies*, vol 17, no 1

ENDS (1993) 'Jury Still Out on Responsible Care', Industry Report No 55, ENDS 222, July

Friedman, M (1963) *Capitalism and Freedom*, Phoenix Books, University of Chicago Press, Chicago

Hartley, R F (1993) *Business Ethics: Violations of the Public Trust*, Wiley, New York

Holloway, R J and Hancock, R S (1968) *Marketing in a Changing Environment*, Wiley, New York

Luthans, F (1985) *Organizational Behaviour* (4th ed), McGraw-Hill, New York

Mintzberg, H (1979) *The Structuring of Organizations*, Prentice-Hall, New York

Welford, R J (1989) 'Growth and the Performance-Participation Nexus: the Case of UK Producer Cooperatives', *Economic Analysis and Workers Management*, vol 23, no 1

Welford, R J (1992) 'Linking Quality and the Environment: A Strategy for the Implementation of Environmental Management Systems', *Business Strategy and the Environment*, vol 1, no 1

Welford, R J (1993) 'Local Economic Development and Environmental Management: An Integrated Approach', *Local Economy*, vol 8, no 2

Westing, J H (1968) 'Some Thoughts on the Nature of Ethics in Marketing', in *Marketing Systems*, R Mayer (ed), 1967 Winter Conference Proceedings, Marketing Association, Chicago

Wheeler, D (1994) 'Auditing for Sustainability: Philosophy and Practice of The Body Shop International' in *Environmental, Health and Safety Auditing Handbook*, McGraw-Hill, Mass

CHAPTER 3

Cahoone, L E (1996) *From Modernism to Postmodernism: An Anthology*, Blackwell, Oxford

Daly, H E (1996) *Beyond Growth: The Economics of Sustainable Development*, MIT Press, Boston, Mass

Freeman, E (1984) *Strategic management: A stakeholder approach*, Pitman Publishing, Boston, Mass

Gray, R H (1994) 'Corporate reporting for sustainable development: accounting for sustainability in 2000 AD', *Environmental Values*, vol 3, no 1, pp17–45

Hawken, P (1994) *The Ecology of Commerce: How Business can Save the Planet*, Weidenfeld and Nicolson, New York

Korten, D C (1995) *When Corporations Rule the World*, Earthscan, London

Porter, M and van der Linde, C (1995) 'Green and Competitive: Ending the Stalemate', *Harvard Business Review*, vol 73, no 5

Schmidheiny, S (1992) *Changing Course: A Global Business Perspective on Development and the Environment*, The MIT Press, Cambridge, Mass

Shiva, V and Bandyopadhyay, J (1989) *The Ecologist*, vol 19, no 3

Welford, R J (1996) *Corporate Environmental Management: Systems and Strategies*, Earthscan, London

Welford, R J (1997) *Hijacking Environmentalism: Corporate Responses to Sustainable Development*, Earthscan, London

CHAPTER 4

Bebbington, J and Gray, R (1996) 'Sustainable Development and Accounting: Incentives and Disincentives for the Adoption of Sustainability by Transnational Organizations' in: Limperg Instituut, *Environmental Accounting and Sustainable Development – The Final Report*, Final Report of the EMAA Workshop, Limperg Instituut, Chartered Association of Certified Accountants, Institute of Chartered Accountants,

Instituut der Wirtschaftsprüfer and Koninklijk Netherlands Instituut van Registeraccountants

Callens, I and Tyteca, D (1995) 'Towards Indicators of Sustainable Development for Firms – Concepts and Definitions', *Fourth International Research Conference of the Greening of Industry Network*, 12–14 November, Toronto, Canada

Eden, S (1994) 'Business, Trust and Environmental Information: Perceptions from Consumers and Retailers', *Business Strategy and the Environment*, vol 3, no 4, pp1–8

Ellger, C and Scheiner, J (1997) 'After Industrial Society: Service Society As Clean Society? Environmental Consequences of Increasing Service Interaction', *The Services Industries Journal*, vol 17, no 4, pp564–79

Gladwin, T N, Klause, T S and Kennelly, J K (1995) 'Beyond Eco-Efficiency: Towards Socially Sustainable Business', *Sustainable Development*, vol 3, no 1, pp35–43

Gray, R H (1994) 'Corporate Reporting for Sustainable Development: Accounting for Sustainability in 2000 AD', *Environmental Values*, vol 3, no 1, pp17–45

Green, K, Morton, B and New, S (1996) 'Purchasing and Environmental Management: Interactions, Policies and Opportunities', *Business Strategy and the Environment*, vol 5, no 3, pp188–97

Irons, K (1994) *Managing Service Companies – Strategies for Success*, Addison-Wesley Publishing Company, Wokingham, England

ISO (1997) *ISO 14031 (Draft International Standard) – Environmental Performance Evaluation Guidelines*, International Organization for Standardization

James, P and Bennett, M (1994) *Environmental-related Performance Measurement in Business: From Emissions to Profit and Sustainability?* Ashridge Management Group Publication

Lundgren, M (1996) *The White Collar Business Ecological Footprints*, School of Business, Stockholm University, Sweden (unpublished)

Morton, B, Green, K, New, S and Miller, C (1997) 'Negotiating Environmental Improvement: The Emerging Role of Environmental Supply Chain Management and NUS Services Ltd', *Business Strategy and the Environment Conference Proceedings*, 18–19 September, Leeds, UK, pp167–72

Normann, R, (1984) *Service Management – Strategy and Leadership in Service Businesses*, John Wiley and Sons, Chichester, UK

Norwegian Ministry of the Environment, (1994) *Symposium: Sustainable Consumption*, Oslo, Norway, 19–20 January

Norwegian Ministry of the Environment, (1995) *Oslo Roundtable Conference on Sustainable Production and Consumption*, Oslo, Norway

Robins, N and Roberts, S (1997) *Changing Consumption and Production Patterns: Unlocking Trade Opportunities*, International Institute for Environment and Development and UN Department of Policy Co-ordination and Sustainable Development, London

Rydberg, T (1995) 'Cleaner Products in the Nordic Countries Based on the Life Cycle Assessment Approach – the Swedish Product Ecology Project and The Nordic Project for Sustainable Product Development', *Journal of Cleaner Production*, vol 3, nos 1–2, pp101–105

Salim, E (1994) 'The Challenge of Sustainable Consumption as Seen from The South', in *Symposium: Sustainable Consumption*, Oslo, Norway, 19–20 January

Shrivastava, P and Hart, S (1995) 'Creating Sustainable Corporations', *Business Strategy and the Environment*, vol 4, no 3, pp154–65

Starik, M, Throop, G M, Doody, J R and Joyce, M E (1996) 'Growing an Environmental Strategy', *Business Strategy and the Environment*, vol 5, no 1, pp12–21

Stead, W E and Stead, J G (1992) *Management for a Small Planet – Strategic Decision Making and the Environment*, Sage Publications, London

van Someren, T C R (1995) 'Sustainable Development and the Firm: Organizational Innovations and Environmental Strategy', *Business Strategy and the Environment*, vol 4, no 1, pp23–33

WBCSD (1996) *Sustainable Production and Consumption – A Business Perspective*, World Business Council for Sustainable Development, Geneva, Switzerland

Welford, R J (1996) *Corporate Environmental Management: Systems and Strategies*, Earthscan, London

Welford, R J (1997) *Hijacking Environmentalism: Corporate Responses to Sustainable Development*, Earthscan, London

Ytterhus, B E and Refsum, S J (1996) *The GRIP Barometer – A Mapping of Environmental Adaptation in the Manufacture of Furniture, Building and Construction, Banking and Insurance, Advertising, Tourism and the Wholesale and Retail Trade*, Center for Research in Environmental Management, The Norwegian School of Management, Norway (unpublished)

CHAPTER 5

Callenbach, E, Capra, F, Goldman, L, Lutz, R and Marburg, S (1993) *EcoManagement: The Elmwood Guide to Ecological Auditing and Sustainable Business*, Berrett-Koehler Publishers, San Francisco

Coddington, W (1993) *Environmental Marketing: Positive Strategies for Reaching the Green Consumer*, McGraw-Hill, New York

Drucker, P F (1973) *Management: Tasks, Responsibilities, Practices*, Harper & Row, New York

EPA (1993) *Status Report on the Use of Environmental Labels Worldwide*, report prepared by Abt Associates for the US Environmental Protection Agency, Washington DC

Kotler, P (1984) *Marketing Management: Analysis, Planning and Control*, Prentice-Hall, New York

Peattie, K (1992) *Green Marketing*, M & E Handbooks, Pitman Publishing, London

UNEP (1991) Global Environmental Labelling: Invitational Expert Seminar, Lesvos, Greece, United Nations Environment Programme/IEO Cleaner Production Programme, New York

Wheeler, D (1993) 'Why Human and Animal Rights Matter in Ecological Policy Making in Europe', paper presented to the Club de Bruxelles Conference on Eco-auditing and Eco-labelling in Europe, Brussels, November

Index

Page numbers in *italics* refer to tables and illustrations.